D1547284

THE
RAINBOW WORLD

THE
RAINBOW WORLD

JAPAN in ESSAYS and TRANSLATIONS

BURTON
WATSON

BROKEN MOON PRESS

Many of these essays were published previously in
Japan: First Impressions, Second Thoughts (copyright ©1984
by Burton Watson, Tokyo, Shubun International Co., Ltd.).
They are reprinted here by permission of the publisher. Some of
these essays also appeared in *Coyote's Journal, Chanoyu
Quarterly, Japan Quarterly,* and *Zero.*

Printed in the United States of America.

ISBN 0-913089-06-0
Library of Congress Catalog Card Number: 89-81099

Cover papercutting, *Heian (Peaceful)*, by Aki Sogabe.
Used by permission of the artist.

Broken Moon Press
Post Office Box 24585
Seattle, Washington 98124-0585 USA

Contents

Translations

Preface

The first piece in this collection, though written many years later, deals with events in the latter part of 1945, when I visited Japan for the first time. The pieces that follow describe happenings as recent as the early 1980s. Thus the collection covers a period of nearly forty years. Readers should keep this fact in mind so that they will not be startled to find mention of a night's lodging and three meals purchased for the sum of 500 yen, or of fish being weighed in a now long-obsolete measure called *momme*. In particular I would ask readers to bear it in mind when reading my remarks in the piece entitled "The Black Fudō" on Japanese and American attitudes toward sex. At the time of writing, 1959, American attitudes seemed to be rather puritanical in comparison to those that prevailed in Japan. Since then, however, American thinking on the subject of sex has undergone radical changes, while the Japanese approach to the subject so far as I can see has remained relatively unchanged. Thus, the positions of the two cultures are now exactly reversed.

Most of these pieces appeared originally in periodicals and are reproduced here in slightly revised form. An earlier and shorter version of the collection was published in Japan in 1984 by Shubunsha International, Tokyo, under the title *Japan: First Impressions, Second Thoughts*.

I would like to thank my friends—Hisao Kanaseki for helping me to put together the original collection, and Sam Hamill for assisting with the arrangements for this American edition.

Burton Watson
Osaka, 1989

Essays

First Impressions

September 20, 1945, when we steamed into Tokyo Bay, was a beautiful clear fall day. A few days earlier we had passed through a violent typhoon, the worst storm I've ever been in at sea. Lockers tipped over with a crash, crockery came hurtling through the air, and the stern rose up so high that the propeller came halfway out of the water with a grinding roar that made the whole ship shiver. It was too rough for the cooks to prepare regular food, so all we had to eat were vats of beans. When the ship made a particularly heavy roll on its side, cascades of them poured down on the feet of the men in the chow line.

But today the sea was calm and bright and the ship moved steadily ahead, sailing into the bay of a country that till a month ago had been our sworn enemy. As we neared the naval base at Yokosuka, we lined up at attention on deck in dress uniforms to present a properly shipshape appearance. A few small fishing boats worked their way along the shore, looking very Oriental and picturesque, and I wondered what Japan would really be like.

I joined the Navy in 1943 at the age of seventeen. I knew I would be drafted at eighteen and I was determined to get into the Navy rather than the Army because I liked ships and water. So I quit high school in the middle of my last year, said good-bye to my friends and went off to volunteer for the Navy. To my great chagrin they rejected me because of poor eyesight. For the next few months I munched vitamins, rolled my eyes and practiced squinting at an eye chart, and on my second try they let me in. That was in April 1943.

I was assigned to duty with the Naval Training School of Photography at Pensacola Naval Air Base in Florida. It was a nice base but I had no interest whatsoever in either airplanes or photography, and so I applied for sea duty. I had visions of sailing through turbulent North Atlantic seas and helping out the British. But my commanding officer said that everyone wanted to go to sea and I would just have to wait my turn.

I was finally assigned to a ship in August 1944, the *Baham*, an old Liberty ship that had been converted into a repair ship. After a shakedown cruise in Chesapeake Bay, we sailed through the Panama Canal and on to Pearl Harbor, where more changes were made on the ship. By this time the naval encounters between Japan and the United States were being fought in the far western part of the Pacific. Instead of sending disabled ships all the way back to the U.S., the Navy decided to set up temporary repair bases in the islands near Japan. We were part of such a base, a floating base that consisted of ships carrying repair crews and equipped with shops for repairing equipment.

For several months after leaving Hawaii we anchored in the bay of Ulithi Atoll in the Caroline Islands. Then in June 1945 we moved to the Gulf of Leyte in the Philippines. There our group broke up, part of the ships going on to the invasion of Okinawa, part withdrawing to Eniwetok in the Marshall Islands to prepare for the invasion of the Japanese home islands. Most of the ships that went to Okinawa were damaged or sunk by kamikaze planes. Luckily our ship was among those that went to Eniwetok, and that was where we were when the war ended.

My job aboard ship was that of communications yeoman. This meant I assisted the communications officer in handling codes and messages, kept track of code publications, and when in port went ashore to draw new publications. My rating was yeoman third class. After basic training I had advanced to seaman second class and then taken the exams for seaman first and later yeoman third. But in order to advance to yeoman second class one had to know shorthand. My halfhearted attempts to teach myself shorthand proved hopeless, so I stayed a yeoman third for the rest of the war.

If you have to take part in a war, I guess there's no better place to be than aboard a naval vessel. You have your food, clothing, and shelter with you at all times and never have to worry about them as long as the ship stays afloat. And you always have the company of your shipmates. You are not required to face the enemy alone or at close quarters—combat, when it occurs, is mechanized and impersonal. Perhaps because of this impersonal nature of our participation in the war against the Japanese, the men on our ship had developed no strong feelings about the enemy. Most of the crew were from the rural South and had never even laid eyes on a Japanese.

The ship's library, small as it was, was fairly well supplied with books on the Allied nations and I had read everything it had to say about China. But there was virtually nothing on Japan. Apparently it had not occurred to anyone that America might actually win the war and that we might end up in Japan. What meager information we had on Japan came largely from an issue of *Life* magazine devoted to the subject. As I recall, it talked at length about the Japanese belief in the divinity of the emperor, a subject that appalled but at the same time rather fascinated Americans at the time. It also related the story of the *Forty-seven Ronin*—I remember there were reproductions of woodblock prints showing scenes from the play—and stressed the enormous importance that the Japanese attached to the avenging of wrongs. This last was a point very much in my mind when I first stepped ashore in Japan to face the people who I knew had every reason to bear me and my country a considerable grudge.

Our ship, after being anchored in Yokosuka harbor for a few days, received permission to send men ashore for liberty. Each crew member was to be allowed one day of liberty a week, the men taking turns going ashore in parties of about thirty. When my day came, I went aft with the others to the paymaster's to change my money—as I recall, we were allowed to change three dollars into yen at the official rate of six yen to the dollar—and then climbed into the liberty boat. In addition to eighteen yen, we were permitted to take two packs of cigarettes with us and whatever gum and candy we wanted. We had been warned that the Japanese were acutely short of food and that we could expect to find nothing to eat or drink on shore, and should not buy anything to eat in the unlikely event we found something for sale. This made candy bars seem like a good thing to take along.

After proceeding by boat up the bay for a considerable time, we were put ashore on a dock in what we were told was Yokohama and began walking toward the downtown area. As I walked along the street from the dock, my first impression, I recall, was one not of strangeness but rather of familiarity. Since leaving Hawaii, the only land areas we had visited had been largely uninhabited beaches and islands—the narrow coral atolls of Ulithi and Eniwetok, with only a few Quonset huts on them, or the palm-lined shores of Leyte and Samar. But here we were in what was obviously a genuine city, fitted out with paved streets and sidewalks, lampposts and rows of trees of the type that grow in the temperate zone. For a moment I thought I was back in America.

But of course it wasn't America, because all around us were Japanese, the men wearing oddly assorted items of old military clothing, the women in faded baggy bloomers of the kind called *mompe.* Contrary to my expectation, they did not look sullen or vengeful, as I am sure I would have been if I had just lost a war, but rather friendly in a cautious and tentative kind of way. And then, as we moved away from the dock area, we could see the terrible destruction all around, the gutted wrecks of buildings, the miles of ash and rubble, with here and there a safe standing stolid and lonely among the ruins. Occasionally we came on parties of men and women working slowly to clear away the debris.

After we had wandered aimlessly along the street for a while, someone in the group suggested we try to go to Tokyo. But which way was Tokyo and how could we get there? From time to time U.S. Army trucks and jeeps sped past us, the only vehicles on the road. We decided to hail a truck and see if we could find out. The driver turned out to be a friendly type and offered to take as many as he could in the open rear of his truck. I hopped up with six or eight others and, waving merrily to people we passed, we bumped along in the morning sun through mile on mile of burned-out factories and suburbs until we reached Tokyo. The driver let us off in a partially bombed area that he said was called Yūrakuchō.

The first thing that struck me here was a loud, confused clip-clopping noise. Large numbers of people were shuffling in a rather listless manner up and down the sidewalks, and almost all of them had on *geta,* or wooden clogs. This was my first introduction to this kind of footgear and the astounding racket it can make in concert, and for a while I stood in wonderment.

Though this was downtown Tokyo, there were almost no stores open, and those that were appeared to have pitifully little to sell. Here and there on the sidewalk, however, enterprising merchants had spread out what few goods they had, a diverse assortment of battered cooking pots, pans, and other secondhand household utensils that looked as though they had been salvaged from the ruins, as well as odds and ends of old clothing. Occasionally someone paused to pick them over. The air was heavy with a kind of musty smell that seemed to exude from the frayed and motley clothing of the passersby or the shabby goods ranged on the sidewalk.

Several of us wandered along until we came to a park. A little way in from the entrance, we arrived before a large stone that to our surprise had words and musical notation on it. We could of course make nothing out of the text in Japanese, but we decided we could at least try singing the notes on the stone, musical notation mercifully being the same East and West. It was our first gesture toward international understanding. We sang the brief melody over two or three times in do-re-mi, gaining confidence and volume as we proceeded. Turning to go, we discovered that a sizable number of Japanese had gathered in a group behind us, watching us intently. They nodded and smiled with surprise, as though the last thing they had expected the American sailors to do was sing the song on the stone. Some months later I learned that the park was called Hibiya and the song was "Kimigayo," the Japanese national anthem.

Wandering a little farther, we came to what we could recognize from photographs we had seen as the main entrance to the imperial palace. Streams of Japanese passed in front of the entrance on one errand or another, a few riding dingy bikes, most of them on foot. Whatever their mode of locomotion, no matter how big a hurry they seemed to be in, they invariably halted abruptly in front of the entrance, turned to face the palace, and made a deep and reverential bow. This time it was our turn to stare in disbelief.

We were afraid we might get lost or for some other reason be unable to return to Yokohama in time to catch the liberty boat back to our ship, a failure that would have had dire consequences. So we hurried back to the street corner where the truck had dropped us and began thumbing for a ride back to Yokohama. Fortunately we reached the dock in plenty of time to get to the boat.

As we pulled out into the bay in the late afternoon, a cold wind began to blow up waves that slapped against the bow. We were wearing white summer uniforms and, having been in the tropics for many months, were wholly unaccustomed to chilly weather. The fact that we had had nothing to eat but candy bars since breakfast added to our discomfort. As evening came on it began to rain. We sat huddled and shivering in the open boat, hoping that Yokosuka was not far off. But the officer in charge of the liberty party couldn't seem to locate our ship among the numerous vessels at anchor in the harbor. It was almost pitch dark when, after hailing various ships and asking directions, he finally found the *Baham* and we sloshed up the gangway and down into our compartment to change clothes. It made a rather cold and bleak ending to my first day ashore in Japan. But, as I reflected, most of the people I had seen on shore that day were no doubt passing an even bleaker evening.

The next few liberties that followed were quite different from this initial excursion. The American commander of the Yokosuka naval base, apparently unwilling to see the war come to an end, gave orders that no personnel under his command were to fraternize in any way with the Japanese or to make any attempt to learn the Japanese language. Naval enlisted men on liberty in Yokosuka, which was where we were now sent for liberty, were to go straight from the liberty-boat landing to the former Japanese Naval Officers' Club, now taken over and made into a PX, drink their allotted three cans of beer, and return directly to the boat landing. SPs were stationed along the route to make certain that no one strayed.

Such a policy, of course, ran directly counter to that of General MacArthur, the boss of the whole show, who had said that Americans and Japanese should be friends. Before long, someone succeeded in calling the attention of *Stars and Stripes,* the Army newspaper in Tokyo, to the discrepancy, and the naval commander was quietly transferred elsewhere. Thereafter we were free to wander around and associate with the Japanese as we pleased. Permission was also given for enlisted men to ride the trains, these previously having been declared off limits to all but commissioned officers. This meant that, put ashore in Yokosuka, we could choose to spend the day there or take a train to Yokohama or elsewhere, provided always that we returned in time to get the liberty boat back to the ship at sundown.

Of course it was hard to do much fraternizing with a people whose language we did not know a word of. The Japanese for their part had been forbidden to study or use English during the war, so even those who had once known some English were understandably rusty. Still, there were ways of expressing simple goodwill without resorting to language.

The children had quickly learned to approach American servicemen with requests for *chokorēto* or *chūingamu.* They were thin and skimpily dressed and usually had sores or scabs on their closely cropped heads and lines of snivel running from their noses. But they were cheerful and appreciative and it was a pleasure to hand out what we had while our supplies lasted. Occasionally older men would approach us timidly, making puffing signs to indicate that they would be grateful for a cigarette, and some of these spoke a little English.

As a result of such encounters, we would sometimes be

invited into a house and offered refreshment. This consisted of weak Japanese tea, sometimes accompanied by a
few dried persimmons or sweet potatoes. In response we
passed around our cigarettes and gum. Gestures and the
drawing of pictures and maps had in most cases to take the
place of conversation, and when that grew tedious, our
hosts would get out the family photo album for us to look
at. It was not what you would call communication on a
very satisfactory level, but everyone seemed to feel that it
was worth working at.

We had no feelings of guilt about the war, since we figured that the Japanese with their Pearl Harbor attack had
brought it on themselves. At the same time it was obvious
that these people had gone through a great deal of suffering
and we were anxious to show that we felt sympathy for
them. As for the Japanese, if they had feelings of hatred or
resentment, they did not show them. When they referred
to deaths or losses incurred in the bombings, they giggled
nervously. This odd laughter disconcerted us greatly at
first until we surmised it was meant to indicate that their
own particular sufferings had been no more than those of
everyone else, and that they did not hold us personally responsible. They seemed determined not to brood on the
past but to get on with whatever the future held for them.

After one or two trips ashore I began carrying a small
black notebook with me when I went on liberty and writing down words I heard in an effort to learn a little Japanese. It was simple enough to acquire nouns merely by
pointing at things, and if I had pursued that course long
enough I suppose I would have ended up like Adam, ca-
pable of naming everything in sight. But it was much more
difficult to get at other parts of speech, and all but impossible to discover the syntax that held them together. Fortunately, the Armed Forces Radio Station in Tokyo began
giving a fifteen-minute Japanese lesson each evening for

the benefit of Occupation personnel, and I became an avid listener. Before long I could manage ordinary greetings, inquire the time or the price of an article, and make a few simple statements. I even learned how to say "Please knock down the price!" though this never had any effect other than to send storekeepers into fits of laughter.

Once we were permitted to ride the trains, I began going to Kamakura on my liberty day. The city had suffered no visible bomb damage, there were historic spots such as the Great Buddha and Hachiman Shrine to see, and it had a few shops open for business. Like most of the Americans in Japan at the time, I was constantly on the lookout for something I could take home as a "souvenir of Japan." We were still limited to three dollars worth of yen at six yen per dollar—when the black-market rate was already thirty or forty yen to the dollar—and were rigorously frisked before we went ashore to make certain we had no more than the authorized two packs of cigarettes. But there was one way that we could augment our meager buying power. We were free to purchase all the clothing we wanted at small stores, and it was easy enough to pass inspection while wearing two pairs of socks or two wool sweaters—on the grounds that the chilly Japanese weather made it necessary, if anyone should happen to ask. Once ashore, the excess layers of clothing could be used as barter for the goods we wanted.

Not, as I have said, that there was all that much for sale. I was not, like some of the men on the ship, in the market for a woman's kimono, since I didn't know anyone who would be likely to appreciate such a gift and it sounded like an expensive and dubious purchase, provided one could even locate one for sale. There was a store in Kamakura that sold beautiful lacquer-ware of the kind called *Kamakura-bori*, but it hardly looked like the kind of place where one could barter for purchases. I confined my attention to little curio and junk shops, where from time to time I found woodblock prints that I liked. They were mostly scenes from kabuki, probably of little value, but light, easy to carry, and pleasant to look at. I have them still.

As the months passed, we learned to find our way around with greater confidence. We learned, for example, that in Yokohama it was possible, and permissible, to buy things to eat in Nankin-machi, the Chinese section of the city, since the Chinese living there received special food rations as members of an Allied nation. You ate in big tents, the buildings in the area having been leveled, and I recall seeing only two dishes for sale, some kind of seashell in broth, and lumps of dough deep-fried in oil and sprinkled with sugar. I never got up the nerve to try the former, but the latter were very tasty indeed. We also discovered a USO in Yokohama where you could get coffee and doughnuts. Men who were looking for a woman found that there were ways to manage that too, though officious U.S. chaplains had made it needlessly complicated by insisting that the Japanese licensed prostitute quarters be declared off limits to Americans.

The high point of my stay in Japan was my trip to Atami. The U.S. Army had taken over a large hotel in the seaside and hot-springs resort town of Atami for the use of its personnel and, in an unusual gesture of interservice generosity, had offered to let the Navy use a few of the rooms. A lottery was held among the men aboard the ships in Yokosuka harbor and I was one of five from my ship to win a trip to Atami.

Joining the winners from the other ships, we took the train to Atami; for some reason which I've forgotten, we rode in a boxcar. It was a clear, cold January day. In the middle of the boxcar a metal can had been placed on the floor, with a fire of sticks burning brightly in it. Two Japanese postmen sat on crates beside it sorting stacks of mail, while the rest of us took turns warming ourselves or looking out the windows at the unfamiliar scenery.

The Atami Hotel, as it was called, turned out to have a fine view out over the Pacific. The meals were all Western style, the food no doubt provided by the Army, but we slept in Japanese-style rooms on bedding spread on the tatami, and also had a chance to try a Japanese-style bath. The greatest delight for me, however, was being able to walk around on land at night. I had not had an opportunity to be on land after dark since leaving Hawaii almost a year before, and it gave me a wonderfully nostalgic feeling to be able to stroll around the streets in the evening and smell the odor of trees and grass on the night air, such a change from the ubiquitous salt smell of the sea. To celebrate my night in town I even ventured into a Japanese movie, but the theater was so packed and the smell of musty clothing so overpowering that I quickly left.

On the third and last day of our stay in Atami, we boarded a bus provided by the hotel and rode over the mountains to another resort, the lakeside town of Hakone. This was my first and only bus ride in Japan, and my first opportunity to see something of the mountain scenery of the country. As we wound and jounced at breathless speed up and down the narrow mountain road, there was much jocular speculation to the effect that the Japanese driver was an ex-kamikaze pilot and that any minute now he would avenge the wrongs done his countrymen by plunging us all over a precipice. It occurred to me that only a few months earlier, I wouldn't have thought such speculations a joking matter.

By this time the Navy had set up a point system, based on the number of months one had been in service and the number one had been on overseas duty, that determined how soon one would be eligible for discharge. I calculated my own points and found that before long I would be able to go back to America and civilian life.

I had heard that the Occupation was badly in need of American civilian employees and that if one were to get discharged in Japan, one would probably have no trouble getting a good job. I was much intrigued with what little I had seen of Japan and eager to learn more about it and have a chance to travel to other places such as Kyoto and Nara. This was the first time in my life I had ever tried to speak a foreign language and I found it great fun, though I had so far failed in all my attempts to get my hands on some kind of textbook for the study of Japanese. Finally, there was a sense of great excitement about the whole Occupation experiment. The country was clearly about as devastated and prostrate as it could be—the only direction it had to go in was up. And the thought of being able to witness that process of slow but gradually accelerating recovery, and perhaps of playing an active part in it, seemed immensely appealing to me.

On the other hand, I had had no more than a high school education, and I was afraid that if I did not go on to college soon, I might somehow miss the opportunity. The GI Bill had been passed, providing funds to cover tuition and books for veterans for a certain length of time, depending upon how long one had been in service. I figured that I could get money for at least four years of higher education, something I would never have been able to afford on my own. So in the end I decided to go back to America when my time came and get discharged there. I had already made up my mind that in college I would major in Chinese and Japanese studies, and that some day I would be back this way again.

Early in February my orders came through. On February 6th, a cold, overcast morning, I and three or four other men from the ship who were being sent home struggled down the gangway with our gear and boarded the small boat that was to take us to the transport ship. Jouncing over the gray waves, I looked back at the *Baham*, which had been my home for almost two years. With the exception of one ex-yeoman I ran into once a few years later at the New York City Center Opera, that was the last I ever saw of all the officers and men I had known aboard it. It was also the last I ever saw of the ship. It was used as a target in the atomic bomb tests at Bikini Atoll later in the year, and I assume was blown to pieces.

The transport, a Coast Guard ship, was so crowded that we had to stand in the chow line for hours and eat standing up so we wouldn't linger over our food. It seemed very peculiar to be aboard a ship that was not mine and on which I had no duties and no identity to speak of. When the weather was nice I sat on the hatch reading or watched the crew shooting at an occasional stray mine that drifted by. But most days were cold and windy and I found it pleasanter to go below and play cards with the other men from my ship. Much of the time I just lay in my sack, staring up at the overhead and wondering when I would get to Japan again.

1981

Dark Slopes

Mount Hiei has dominated Kyoto history as it dominates the Kyoto landscape. In fact, it is one reason for the location of the city, forming as it does a towering wall on the northeast, the direction from which come all evil spirits. In 788 the monk Dengyō Daishi established a small temple on its summit and, shortly after, the new capital was laid out in the mountain's protective shade. The temple grew with the city and Mount Hiei became a flourishing center of learning and religious activity. The original cluster of halls multiplied until temples covered the long summit and ran down the sides to the valleys north of Kyoto and the shore of Lake Biwa which borders the mountain on the east. With perhaps a bit of poetic license, the priests of Mount Hiei boasted of their three thousand temples.

Although I had been up the mountain many times by the cable cars that ascend its eastern and western slopes, I was curious once to try the trip on foot. Setting off one November morning by the trail called Mica Lane, I trudged toward the summit through cool valleys and along ridges waist-deep in grass, looking hopefully for some sign of the three thousand temples. But I found no trace of the passing of time except a single stone marker recording some ancient battle that had swept for a day over the steep hillside, leaving its dead for the stone to remember.

By noon I reached Enryaku-ji, the main group of buildings that perches overlooking Lake Biwa. This is the heart of the sanctuary, the part of the mountain familiar to all tourists who follow the well-worn road from the head of one cable to the other. These great red and black chapels, however, towering over the site of Dengyō Daishi's original temple, are no more than late descendants of the Heian halls, separated from their ancient predecessors by a curtain of darkness.

Mount Hiei had prospered under the patronage of the Kyoto aristocracy, but this very prosperity proved to be its undoing. Wealth attracted to the temples the riffraff that an earlier austerity had been careful to exclude. Women came to live on the holy ground where no female had been permitted. The monks began to meddle in politics, making raids against rival temples, burning and massacring in defiance of all Buddhist law. At the slightest provocation they would shoulder the sacred carriage of the Shinto god of the mountain and roar down upon the capital, terrorizing the court and citizens. "The Mountain," as Kyoto people referred to it, grew to be a major political power, and the little temple founded to keep the devils out of the city became its greatest affliction.

But arrogance and evil, as the priests might have known, have their own reward. After centuries of luck, the temples managed to get on the wrong side of a political quarrel. One autumn evening in 1571 the military adventurer Oda Nobunaga marched with his army up from Lake Biwa to put an end to the nuisance on the mountain. Beginning at the north end, he worked his way south, burning every building and killing every human being he encountered. By morning some sixteen hundred men, women, and children lay dead and the mountain was a smoking ruin.

The peace that followed saw the reconstruction of a few of the main halls, but the Tokugawa shoguns, fearful of a revival of the mountain's formidable power, clamped strict limitations on the number of buildings and size of land holdings. Today some twenty chapels dot the summit where a small and chastened clergy continue the ancient ceremonies of the sect. But the melancholy work of that autumn night still seems to hang like a shadow over the silent mountain forests.

I found a room in the lodge attached to the temple, left my things, and set out to visit a group of buildings on the eastern slope. Descending flights of stone steps between halls built out over the hill, I came upon a middle-aged priest in white robes directing a group of workmen. He greeted me cheerfully and guided me around the temple to see the repairs he was making. It grew late, the workmen finished for the day, and we all went to a building higher up where the priest lived.

"Last year I built that," he said, pointing with pride to a small new chapel on our way, "and before that I repaired this building where I live. I'm very good at raising money," he added. His face was thin and ascetic but he spoke a frank, hearty Japanese that suggested a business executive. This was the spirit, I thought, that first covered these hills with three thousand temples.

"I have no wife," he continued after we had entered his house and were seated, "and so I work on the temples on top of the mountain. Since the Restoration, priests have been allowed to marry but they cannot keep their wives up here. So they have two temples, one on top of the mountain and one at the foot. They live down below with their families and come up at dawn on the first cable to perform services. But if they get a little money their wives make them put it into the temple down below, so these up here fall into ruin. That's why wives are a bad thing!" he concluded with sweeping generalization.

The house we were in was built on a fold of the hill, the windows that ran along one side facing across a narrow ravine to a bank of pines and cypresses. A corner of Lake Biwa shone far in the distance. "Were there other temples around here in old times?" I asked. "There were six right over there where you're looking," he replied. "In all these folds—wherever there was water—there were temples."

I wanted to ask about the burning of the mountain, but I was uncertain whether to broach the subject with historical detachment or feign a tone of indignation. "They were very bad in those days," continued the priest of his own accord. "Not priests at all but a bunch of worthless ruffians." He paused a while. "Things are different now, though. We have only a few men but they are serious and hard-working. The number is growing, we are beginning to revive. You come back in forty years and you will see a big difference. I will have those six temples over there rebuilt!"

He got out a bottle of sake and told the old woman who acted as housekeeper to warm some. "All presents from parishioners," he said, waving at the sake and some cartons of cigarettes. "I ask for nothing for myself—people just bring me things. If you have no desires," he added in a confiding tone, "all things will be given to you."

The housekeeper brought the sake. Two boys in student uniforms appeared at the door, knelt and announced with formal bows that they had just returned from school. Like most of the boys studying for the priesthood, they lived on top of the mountain and went each day to the Buddhist college at the foot.

A cold wind blew in from the lake. I sat drinking the hot wine and wondering what satisfaction one might find living in a place like this. The Japanese, forced by the mountainous terrain of their narrow islands to live piled on top of each other in valleys, have always idolized solitude and silence, the two things they lack most in their daily lives. The poet-priests of old Japan in particular wrote endless verses on the joys of their mountain-top retreats, one of which came to mind as I gazed across the ravine:

A supper of pine flowers,
monk's robes of chestnut dye—
what dream does the world hold
to lure me from these dark slopes?

I thought I saw, perhaps, what the poet meant.

"The people at the lodge will be worried," I said, rising.

"Have some more sake!" the priest commanded and, going to the next room, he shattered the illusion of antiquity I had been carefully nurturing by picking up a telephone and dialing. "The foreigner is at my place," he announced with authority, "and will be somewhat delayed." He hung up and returned. Another priest appeared and the three of us sat drinking and talking of the past and future of the mountain while the green slopes outside the window turned to black and then silvered in the light of a newly risen moon. After some time I managed to excuse myself, threaded my way back unsteadily to the top of the mountain, ate my vegetarian supper and went to bed.

The glare of the sun rising over the lake woke me early the next morning. I dressed quickly and went for a walk. Through the groves of tall evergreens sounded the clop of wooden knockers and the drone of chanting: morning services in all the chapels had begun. I climbed to a peak of the mountain where I could look down at Kyoto in the west. Kyoto people have been notorious through the centuries of Japanese history for their frugal ways. In the old days they confined their breakfast to a thin rice gruel, and it was said that if you stood on the top of Mount Hiei at dawn and listened carefully you could hear a distinct buzz rising from the capital, the sound of thousands of thrifty citizens slurping their morning porridge. The city this morning had disappeared under a blanket of thick fog. Only the tops of the western hills were visible like islands floating over a white sea. I could hear no buzz of porridge-eating. Kyotoites of today have found it is even cheaper to eat bread and milk.

I returned to the lodging house, ate my own breakfast of bean soup and pickles, paid my 500 yen bill for a night's lodging and meals, and started out for Yokawa, a group of temple buildings at the north end of the mountain. As I turned off the main road that leads to the Kyoto cable, a party of old ladies wearing dark kimonos and pilgrims' badges appeared over the crest of the hill and clambered down the stony path in their precarious wooden clogs, laughing and joking with all the shrill abandon that is forbidden to proper Japanese women in their youth. They were the last people I saw until I reached Yokawa.

For a while my path wound among a scattering of chapels—the Hall of the Pure Land, the great Hall of Shaka, resplendent in vermilion among the dark pines, the tiny Emerald Hall, the only building on the mountain that escaped the burning. Morning services were over and the chapels were silent. The students had locked up and gone to school; the priests, if my friend of the day before was to be believed, had taken the cable car back down to the world of families and desire. The mountain narrowed and the trail threaded back and forth along its thin spine, overlooking first the deep-folded hills north of Kyoto, then turning to follow the bank of pines that dipped to the shore of Lake Biwa.

Around noon I reached Yokawa, a cluster of buildings grouped around a terrace of stone, the site of the old Central Hall. The hall itself had burned down in a lightning storm fifteen years ago, firing the stones of its foundation so that they split and crumbled into odd shapes.

I found the priest in charge, a young man in dark robes. He greeted me with wistful surprise. "No one ever comes at this time of the year," he explained. "I'm the only person here and I generally don't see anyone but the postman until spring." He led me to a sitting room and disappeared. After a long time he returned with a bowl of soup which I ate with the lunch of cold rice I had brought from the lodge. "I don't eat lunch myself," he assured me. "It's a lot of bother and I'm too busy." I asked in surprise what could keep him so occupied. "I chant sutras," he replied. "All day."

He guided me around the buildings, a group of weathered gray halls scattered among the bright autumn maples, murmuring an apology for their dilapidated condition. "I wish I had time to do more," he said in a sad voice. I asked about the history and geography of this end of the mountain, but most of my questions he answered with a listless confession of ignorance. I began to consider whether my impressions of the day before—the conviviality, the sake, the hearty optimism—were to be trusted. Yokawa appeared very different, as though the north and south ends of the mountain were playing out the opposite phases of a cycle of nascence and decay. Was this, I wondered, the true effect of mountain solitude upon the mind? Were these perhaps the real "dark slopes" of the poem?

We had circled the grounds and arrived in front of the stone terrace. "This leads to the lake," he said, indicating a wide path that sloped off through the trees. "This is the road Oda Nobunaga came by—when all this was burned down." He waved his hand in the direction of the crumbling stones with a vagueness that suggested he hardly distinguished between the sixteenth-century general who turned the mountain to ashes and the lightning that destroyed the Central Hall fifteen years ago.

"But I want to go back down the Kyoto side," I reminded him uneasily. "Oh," he said thoughtfully. "I think there's some road that goes to the village of Ōhara." He thought a while longer. "Do you see that little graveyard over there?"

he asked, pointing among the trees. "The path leads off from there." He paused and, apparently unable to think of anything further to say about the road, added in a pleasant voice, "That's the graveyard where I will be buried when I die."

I thanked him and hurried off in the direction he had indicated, hoping to get down the mountain and back to Kyoto well before dark. But the path was faint and uncertain and the stone markers that should have told me the way had fallen on their sides so that their guiding arrows pointed meaninglessly up into the air. It was deep twilight by the time I finally reached Ōhara.

1956

The Rainbow World

The section of Kyoto called Demachi lies in what used to be the northeast corner of the capital, overlooking the juncture of the Kamo and Takano rivers. As the name indicates, it was the point at which people "left the city" on their way to Kitashirakawa, Ichijō-ji, or Ōhara, and to which peddlers from those villages brought their goods for sale, though the city now fans out far beyond it. The houses are mostly in the dark, massive style of architecture typical of the older sections of Kyoto. With their sanded black walls and expanses of reddish-brown wooden grill, they have a fortress-like air of permanence which sets them off from the flimsier structures across the river or the semi-Western-style houses of Shimogamo to the north.

In spite of its antique setting, however, life in Demachi manages to keep pretty well up with the times. Neon signs decorate the store fronts, fluorescent lights cast a cold glare over the brown interiors, and the little coffee shops and drinking stands along its side streets provide background music of Beethoven or Presley as the mood demands. It was in one of the latter where I was quietly drinking sake one evening that I suddenly found myself involved in a particularly knotty example of intercultural exchange.

A phonograph operated by one of the girls at the counter had been soothing us with a variety of sad ballads when a man next to me asked for something in the way of a Japanese folk song. The proprietress, a motherly type in a dark kimono, turned to the girl. "Put on 'Shōjō-ji,'" she said. "The one by Eartha Kitt."

I had first heard this record when I returned to New York in 1955 after a stay in Japan. The song itself, a children's song about raccoon dogs dancing in the moonlight, I had heard many times in Japan. But at the time I was not aware that Miss Kitt had recorded a version of it.

I was living in an apartment in lower Manhattan, a so-called cold-water flat. (The term cold-water flat, I might explain, is technically an anachronism, since New York law now requires that all places where people are actually living must be provided with hot running water. But the distinction between hot and cold water, so clear to the Japanese that they employ two entirely different words for them, tends to be lost on many New York apartment house superintendents, and if you attempt to enlighten them on the point, they are apt to retaliate by sending live steam up through the pipes at you.) My neighbors in the building were mostly Greeks, Czechs, or Italians of the first generation. I was hence quite accustomed to hearing almost any variety of European national music coming from their rooms. But the sudden strains of Japanese raccoon dogs drifting down the stairwell as I returned one evening were at once so familiar and yet so out of place that I listened for some time before I realized that the song was indeed the one I had heard so often in Japan and the singer was Eartha Kitt, and that it was issuing in a quite ordinary manner from the radio in the apartment of the elderly Greek couple across the hall.

This, then, was the song, exported to Miss Kitt and re-imported to Demachi, that we were now hearing. A chorus of girls chanted in Japanese in the background but Miss Kitt, in spite of her famed linguistic versatility, had chosen to do her part in English. Taking a hint from the word *make-ru-na*, an injunction in the original to the raccoon dogs not to be outdone in their dancing, the American arranger had invented some nonsense for her to sing about "macaroons" and other good things to eat.

The proprietress and the girl at the phonograph sang along sweetly on the chorus, but their faces puckered into frowns of concentration when we came to the macaroons. "We can't understand this part," said the proprietress in her thick Kyoto accent. "What's she saying?"

I listened to the words Miss Kitt was crooning.

"Jelly beans," I replied and, as I had feared, drew a blank.

"A kind of candy made of *zeri*," I explained. This seemed to satisfy them. We practiced saying the word over together two or three times.

"And what comes after that?"

"I forget. You'll have to play the record over," I said. The girl obligingly set the needle back to the beginning.

"There, there! What's that word?"

I looked apprehensively at their bright, expectant faces. "Pink spumoni," I said. It was some time before we cleared that up.

It is no wonder that the ladies were momentarily thrown off by the sudden introduction of jelly beans and pink spumoni into their environment. Indeed, it is hardly surprising that the Japanese sometimes find themselves baffled even by the sound of their own language, considering the prodigious number of non-Japanese words that have entered it in recent years. Listening to the speech of Japanese intellectuals, with its heavy interpolations of English and other foreign elements, like lumps in a pudding, one wonders how they put up with it. One can only suppose that, in spite of its odd sound, this new potpourri is for the speakers incomparably richer and more satisfying than the leaner speech of former times.

Japanese are fond of referring to themselves as a backward nation (though the papers have declared the term definitely out-of-date). But in the degree to which they have succeeded in familiarizing themselves with the cultures of the rest of the world and fusing them with their own, they are far ahead of most other countries. It is easy enough to harp on the superficiality of much of the resultant cosmopolitanism, but rather pointless, since no understanding of anything new can ever begin by being profound. In late Tokugawa and Meiji times the Japanese set about in great haste to inform themselves of the content and background of Western culture, of which they had previously been relatively ignorant, and Western students of the period are appropriately amused by the quaint errors and misconceptions of their novitiate. But that era of awkwardness has long since ended, while the West, in its corresponding knowledge of East Asian culture, has just started to cope with essentials. It will be a long time, we may be certain, before the average Westerner is prepared to deal with anything as recherché as the Japanese for pink spumoni, or whatever its Eastern equivalent may be.

Everyone seems to agree that the world is fated to become one. Whether, like the advent of interplanetary travel, one regards this as a happy prospect or not is, I suppose, a matter of temperament. Certainly the idea of oneness has about it a disquieting suggestion of sameness. Music and art of the so-called "modern" variety have in fact already achieved a style, or range of styles, that are depressingly alike the world over, and Huxley predicts that the manners and customs of nations will likewise in time become so uniform that there will no longer be any point in travel. It is indeed possible that the world of the future may eventually resolve into the muddy sort of gray that children end up with when they perversely mix together all the colors in a box of paints. But more likely, or at least before that happens, it seems we are destined to go through a delightful rainbow phase such as the Japanese are now entering, where all will be not sameness but variety, where things will not be blurred but merely juxtaposed with arresting incongruity—Chopin against samisen music, Bashō against T. S. Eliot, Mary Baker Eddy against Zen—and all the colors will vibrate with a new brilliance.

The girl at the phonograph had obliged us with a further selection of chansons and calypso ballads and we were back to Eartha Kitt and the raccoon dogs. The proprietress hummed along brightly as she poured my sake for me.

"Jelly beans!" she sang out when we got to the part in English, smiling confidently as though she had been eating them all her life.

"Pink spumoni!" echoed the girl at the phonograph, and beyond the dark roofs of Demachi I could see the great, parti-colored world of the future bobbing merrily into view on the horizon.

1958

Mibu Kyōgen

After four or five years in Kyoto I have ceased to bother with most of the annual festivals that are a chief delight to newcomers. Of course, in a city of this size, unless you make a point of avoiding them, you are apt to start off on some errand and suddenly find yourself inadvertently caught up in a festive procession. But this is perhaps even pleasanter than setting out with that purpose, since inadvertent festivals, like unpremeditated pleasures, are usually the best. There is one yearly event, however, that I try not to miss: the Mibu Kyōgen.

Mibudera, the temple where the *kyōgen*, or "farces," are held, is located in the western section of the downtown area—the industrial slums of the city, insofar as Kyoto has enough industry to warrant the adjective. Ever since the capital was laid out in the eighth century in the form of a neat rectangle patterned after the Chinese capital at Ch'ang-an, the western sector seems to have been unpopular. It was too barren and exposed, the water was bad, the inhabitants were menaced by wild beasts—a number of reasons have been offered to explain its lack of appeal. The government took measures to confine the inhabitants within the area it had marked out and make them dispose themselves with appropriate symmetry on either side of the main street leading to the palace in the north. But the aristocracy insisted upon crossing the boundary of the Kamo River and residing on the cool slopes of the eastern hills, drawing the life of the city with them, and soon the tidy geometry of the city planners had been effaced by a great bulge in the east. Through the years the citizens continued to drift irresponsibly out of their Chinese rectangle and the western wards reverted to farmland, which they remained until the end of the last century, when population growth caused the city to expand in all directions. Mibudera, which used to stand out in the fields, is now hemmed in by Meiji-period slums and dyeing and weaving factories and, far from happening upon it inadvertently, you must leave the main street and walk down a narrow alley and across railroad tracks to reach its low gray gates.

The temple is reputedly some thousand years old, though it has been destroyed innumerable times by fire and the present buildings date from the early 1800s, a collection of weathered halls, dilapidated like the neighborhood, surrounded by a crumbling mud wall. Since it is not obliged, like the better-known temples of Kyoto, to look aesthetically pleasing for the sake of tourists, it can afford to cater to the more practical needs of the district. The compound, dusty and almost treeless, doubles as a playground for swarms of racing children and, at least during the time the farces are held, is dotted with candy and toy stands and fortunetellers' stalls. Perched atop a great mound of stones beside the main hall is a statue of the patron deity of the temple, Lord Jizō, the protector, appropriately enough, of little children. In one corner is a pond covered with emerald scum.

The farces are performed on a sort of roofed balcony, constructed on the general plan of a Noh stage, that projects high above the ground from one of the halls. When I first used to go to see them, there was a long, ramshackle shed, built on stilts and separated from the stage by an open court, in which the spectators sat on straw mats and viewed the performance. This has since been replaced by an elevated concrete hall, on the outside attempting unhappily to imitate the lines of the older wooden buildings, but on the inside looking more like a Sunday-school room in a small-town Baptist church. Now we sit on benches along the side of the room and look across the court at the shabby stage, which seems, beside the concrete monster, to have receded sharply in time, while in the hall behind the benches, as in Sunday-school rooms, innumerable little children dash wildly about. The plays are held during the last days of April, when the leaves of the trees are a bright new green and gusts of wind billow the robes of the actors and whirl up clouds of dust in the courtyard.

The origin of the farces is obscure. An old tradition relates them to the *Dainembutsu,* the street-corner revival meetings of the Middle Ages in which the priests led the people in invocations of the Buddha's name accompanied by singing and dancing, though some scholars question the derivation. In any event, by middle-Tokugawa times the temple possessed a repertory of half-a-dozen original farces which it performed each year, and later other plays were taken over and adapted from the Noh drama.

The plays are pure pantomime; there is no dialogue, but only a brassy bell, a drum, and occasionally a flute to accompany the action. In order to convey the plot, the actors must make bold, sweeping gestures, repeated several times to be sure that the audience has grasped each step in the development. Incongruously, a loudspeaker has recently been added, droning away to make doubly certain that we are all following. "The wine the lady is giving him to drink is really poison. You will note that she did not drink her share, but threw it away while he was not watching . . ." (Idiot! We *saw* the man hold up his sleeve to indicate he wasn't looking and watched while the lady whooshed the sake bowl upside down and dashed the imaginary wine to the ground!)

The actors are all men, amateurs from the neighborhood, dressed in shabby robes, like the costumes of a Christmas pageant that has not been refurbished in a great many years. Their faces are covered by masks fixed to their heads with swathes of white bandage. Obviously there are elements here that outwardly resemble the Noh drama— the shuffling walk of the actors, the masks, the drum and flute, even, as I have said, the plots of some of the plays. But it is the Noh stripped of all its elegance and mystery, the court drama transported to the street corner. The gestures are absurdly exaggerated, the bell clanks noisily in the background, a lady in ill-fitting robes lifts an arm and reveals a grubby masculine elbow, someone gets turned around in a piece of business and has to be given whispered directions in sight of the audience—all this, however, not because the plays are being performed by inept amateurs, you feel, but because their very essence is a kind of hearty crudeness that would be destroyed by anything slick or suave (as it is already being destroyed by the loudspeaker and the concrete Sunday-school room).

In most countries the more primitive forms of drama die out as they are replaced by later developments. But in Japan, perhaps because of the Japanese fondness for variety, they all live on into the present. Each stage in the evolution of the dramatic art, arrested at its highest point and hardened in a mold of tradition, not only survives but continues to draw appreciative audiences. The Mibu farces hardly represent a very high level of artistic achievement. Kyoto people call them *ahokusai*, meaning "foolish," and yet continue to go to see them year after year. Their charm no doubt consists in this very primitiveness, the nostalgic foolery of an earlier age. They are rather what I have always imagined the old English mystery plays to be, or the sort of dumb show and mummery Europeans must have watched at dusty medieval fairs. Perhaps because of their general shoddiness, they look much older than most of the supposedly "ancient" festivals of Kyoto.

Are the farces, then, like the English mystery plays, intended to instruct the unlettered in religious doctrine or point some pious moral? Having posed the question, I must disclaim any ability to answer it. Many of the pieces illustrate the effectiveness of earnest prayer, some display the patron deity, Lord Jizō, in the act of vanquishing demons, and all seem to have some connection with religious rites or observances. But they also contain a large amount of pure horseplay. Is the point of the drama the pious element or the horseplay that surrounds it? Or, to turn to the parallel I have suggested above, is the focus of the English mystery plays the lusty brawl between Mr. and Mrs. Noah and the buffoonery of Mak and the Shepherds, or is it the soberer themes of God's grace and the redemption of mankind? I doubt that the English who wrote the mystery plays or the Japanese who devised these farces could have said. Slapstick alone would hardly have accorded with the religious occasions that were the excuse for the dramas, while pure preaching would have bored the spectators; by combining the two, they pleased everyone. It is only in recent centuries, when true religious ardor has waned, that people have grown self-conscious about the outward semblance of piety, and come to regard the old marriage of buffoonery and religion as incongruous, if not actually shocking. Englishmen of a later age, distinguishing sternly between piety and horseplay, banned the mystery plays. The Mibu farces continue, I suppose, because there are still people in Kyoto who happily do not insist upon the distinction.

One of the oldest and most famous of the farces belonging exclusively to Mibudera is that entitled *Oketoru*, or *Drawing Water*. To illustrate what I have been saying, let me outline the plot. A young lady named Teruko comes each day to the temple to pay her respects to Lord Jizō. Dipping water meticulously from the pond (represented by the open court), she balances the pail on three fingers and, to the accompaniment of the flute, executes an odd bobbing dance, while her feet and free hand describe circles in the air. (According to my program, the "circles" are in fact Sanskrit symbols representing the mystic workings of the Buddha, though without explanation this would hardly be apparent.)

The Rake, a stock character in the farces, wearing a grotesque chocolate-colored mask, enters and begins to annoy her with his attentions. She attempts to dampen his ardor with the water from her pail, but after he has looped a sash about her neck and is threatening to strangle her, she adopts a more friendly attitude. She instructs him in the figures of her sacred dance, which he bunglingly imitates, and soon the two are cavorting merrily about the stage.

The Rake's wife appears, a gawky woman wearing an *otafuku* mask—great puffy cheeks, a tiny nose, the Japanese representation of supreme homeliness. She charges on the couple and showers them with blows until her husband kicks her into a corner. He and the maiden try to escape, but the wife pursues and for a time the two women play tug-of-war with their chocolate-faced prize. The wife is once more overpowered and tossed into a heap, while the guilty pair flee. She picks herself up in a rage and, taking out a mirror and a box of powder, decides to try the aid of cosmetics. She makes motions of daubing her face with powder, she pounds at her protruding cheeks, she pulls at her diminutive snub nose—but it is no use. Flinging the mirror aside, she buries her face in her hands and, shaking with sobs, exits slowly from the stage.

The loudspeaker, unable to find any point in the action that appears to require elucidation, has been discoursing irrelevantly on the history of the temple, drowning for a while the monotonous clanging of the bell. A child has fallen off the bench behind me and landed on its head. In an effort to quiet its howling, the mother directs its attention to the stage. "Look, look! The man is kicking his wife!" For a moment the child is distracted, while a gust of wind whirls dust and candy papers from the ground below. "Oh, poor thing—now she's crying!" exclaims the mother. Perhaps because he has grasped the moral of the play, or perhaps only because he has inadvertently been reminded of what it was he wanted to do, the child bursts out once more in a loud wail.

1959

Kiyomori and
the Memory of the Past

In all but name alone, the ruler of Japan in the middle of the twelfth century was Taira no Kiyomori, the strong-willed head of the Heike, or Taira family. By defeating his rivals of the Minamoto clan and ousting the Fujiwaras from their position of supremacy at court, he succeeded in seizing all military and civil power, while the emperor remained, as before, a pawn in the hands of his contentious barons. When, shortly after Kiyomori's death in 1181, the tables were abruptly turned and the Heike driven from their homes in Kyoto and hounded to defeat by the resurgent Minamotos, they left behind them in the capital a scattering of sad remains and a memory of evanescent glory. Of the remains, one may still see in a temple on the eastern hills of Kyoto the robe of Kiyomori's grandson, Emperor Antoku, proclaimed ruler in 1180 at the age of two and drowned five years later at the great sea battle of Dan-no-ura; in a nunnery north of the city, a statue of his mother, Kenreimon-in, consort of Emperor Takakura; and in another temple in the district called Rokuhara, a statue of Kiyomori himself, the man who led the Heike to power and who, by his arrogance and evil, paved the way for their sudden downfall. As for the memory, it quickly became the inspiration for a long romance, the *Heike monogatari*, or *Tale of the Heike*, written in a rich and strongly rhythmical language and recording in dramatic detail the meteoric career of the Tairas, which indeed is the chief reason that most people today have heard of Kiyomori and his heirs, or care. When all their earthly power and possessions had vanished, literature alone preserved the fame of the unfortunate family.

Rokuhara, the site of the old Taira headquarters in Kyoto, is an area east of the Kamo River, bounded by Matsubara-dōri on the north and the Kyoto Museum on the south. In Kiyomori's time it was a complex of mansions and parks, containing some five thousand houses of the Heike, though nothing at all remains of these. The Minamotos, after wiping out the Taira family, occupied the site; and their successors to power, the Hōjō regents, who controlled the Kamakura shogunate, used it for their government offices in the capital. All traces of these likewise are gone, obliterated by the frequent conflagrations that raged over the area. Rokuharamitsu-ji, or the Temple of the Six Paramitas, founded in 963, long before the rise of the Tairas, and situated in the northern part of the district, is in fact the only thing that remains from the ancient Rokuhara. The present hall of the temple, constructed in 1363, is one of the oldest buildings in Kyoto, and it is here that the statue of Kiyomori is preserved.

I came on the temple by accident one day as I was wandering home from an exhibition at the Kyoto Museum. An unimposing hall, hemmed in by a primary school and rows of houses, its drab exterior resembles those of countless other run-down temples on Kyoto's side streets. I very nearly walked by without stopping. When I changed my mind and asked the priest at the entrance to show me around, he led me over shining black floors to the inner part of the sanctuary. In the dim light, the wood of the hall shone a rich, velvety brown, flecked here and there with the peeling remnants of frescoes. When the temple was new, the pillars and ceilings must have been covered with gaudy greens and vermilions. That so little remains is impressive evidence of the age of the building.

The priest, pointing to the statue in a curtained recess

of the main altar, began to rehearse the history of the temple. "Some one thousand years ago, Saint Kūya, the founder of the temple, carved this statute of the eleven-headed Kannon . . ."

For some reason, this method of indicating dates, so much used by Japanese guides, has always bothered me. Logically it would seem the most natural thing to indicate points in time in this fashion by relating them to our own position, as we indicate distances by saying "three hundred miles east of here." And yet, perhaps because we do not, and never can, have any direct personal experience of great periods of time, as we have these days of great distances, statements such as "a thousand years ago" never really penetrate the mind. In the end, all the past is equally far away, and the Middle Ages, the Heian period, the thirteenth century are no more than the names of legendary continents, contiguous perhaps, but each as inaccessible as the next from the shore on which we stand. Confronted with a date in the distant past, therefore, we must scurry around in our minds until we have located it in one or another of these imaginary lands, and only then do we feel at ease to stand back and listen to the account of what happened at that time.

The priest's explanations became increasingly complicated. The Tairas had lived in the neighborhood, it seemed, and after them the Minamotos, and for a while I knew where I was. Then the dates began again. "Some three hundred and fifty years ago—*Ima kara oyoso sambyaku gojū nen mae . . .* " Being very poor at figures, I began surreptitiously counting on my fingers: "1959, 1859, 1759 . . ." Halfway through, I discovered he had finished the sentence. We rounded the side of the hall in silence and drew up abruptly before the statue of Taira no Kiyomori.

The statue is seated on a dais behind the altar, backed by a gold screen and illumined dramatically by a spotlight from below. It is made of lacquer, and its skin is black and dusty like a mummy's.

Kiyomori is portrayed as a pleasant-faced old man with shaved head, wearing the robes of a priest and holding in his hands a roll of the scriptures. This may seem a surprising pose for a man renowned in his lifetime as a ruthless tyrant, who was responsible for the destruction of several famous temples and the slaughter of their monks. As my guide explained, however, in 1168, because of a serious illness, Kiyomori took the tonsure, so that the title of *Nyūdō*, or Lay Priest, was thereafter prefixed to his court title of prime minister. However his life belied it, the artist has therefore generously permitted the dictator to be viewed by posterity in the garb of a religious man, his hands fondling the sacred writings, his keen eyes absorbed in their words of wisdom.

The literary monument to Kiyomori, the *Tale of the Heike*, is similarly clothed in Buddhist robes, beginning as it does with the famous passage on the bell of the Gion Temple that tolls the impermanence of all things, and harping on the theme of karmic retribution. But, as in the case of the statue, it occurred to me that the garb may be a bit deceptive, or at least misleading.

To begin with, since Japan received Buddhism from the continent at the same time it received the art of writing, all Japanese literature in the past has of necessity been colored by Buddhist ideas to some extent, with the exception perhaps of the Shinto-minded legends and songs that had already taken shape before the introduction of writing. Japanese writers, no matter how profane their subject, could never wholly escape the effects of their Buddhist heritage, and it is not always easy to differentiate in their works between religious conviction and mere literary convention.

I do not mean by this that one need doubt the sincerity

of the author (or authors) of the *Tale of the Heike* when he voices traditional Buddhist sentiments, any more than one need doubt the sincerity of Kiyomori in taking religious vows. Yet the presence of such passages in the *Tale* is hardly justification for regarding it as a religious work, a sermon on Buddhist philosophy, as some critics have done. Buddhist philosophy teaches that existence is a dream, that all our commonplace notions of form and color, time and space, are phantoms of the mind. Such a concept, however, though it may be made the subject of philosophical exposition, is an all but impossible subject for literature since, like the Christian concept of God's omnipotence, it defies expression in terms that are meaningful to the human imagination. To be truly Buddhist, or Christian for that matter, literature, it would seem, must be either devotional—descriptions of the transcendental world and exhortations to the mind or the soul to journey there, or hagiographical—records of the lives of men who have succeeded in making that journey.

The *Tale of the Heike,* taken as a whole, is patently neither of these. The author's interest, far from being otherworldly, is centered squarely upon this world; and instead of despising its deeds and personalities, he seems desperate to record them in all possible verisimilitude. The chief beauty of the *Tale,* in fact, lies in its vivid and moving descriptive passages: panoramas of burning temples and battle mayhem, quiet scenes of men and women in lonely gardens, accounts to the point of tedium of the precise hue and cut of each character's armor or robes. Japanese literary sentiment is in fact too deeply wedded to the particular—particular seasons, particular places, particular sounds and smells—to make the idea of a sweeping negation of reality even thinkable. The characters of the *Tale,* rather than abandoning the world, cling tightly to their familiar places and ways of life. Driven from them by a force beyond their control, their lives are reduced to an endless series of bitter partings and tearful farewells.

The principal concern of the author of the *Tale* is to trace out in time the changing fortunes of the Taira family, the working out of its karma, a great arc curving ineluctably downward from riotous power to the last cry of defeat, within which are described smaller arcs of the fortunes of Kiyomori's opponents. And at frequent intervals, he pauses to reflect upon the course of his narrative and call up parallels from the ancient history of Japan and China. For the *Tale* is, after all, a work of the historical imagination. From the point of view of the author, its value lies not in the fact that, as in a novel, these things *might* have happened, but that they *did* happen, probably within the writer's own memory. So appalled were the Japanese by the spectacle of Kiyomori's unbridled tyranny and the rapidity with which his family fell from power and were driven to final defeat off the shore of southern Honshu, that they felt compelled to make an immediate record of the event in all its striking and pathetic detail.

True, this is not the austere chronicle we are accustomed to having handed us in the name of history. Its surface has been colored by imagination, its outlines softened by nostalgia and moulded by art. But the bones of the narrative are historical fact. Like the language of the *Tale*, which is heavy with Chinese phrases and allusions, the work is essentially less Buddhist than Chinese in inspiration, for it is the Chinese, of all people, who have been most concerned with the mapping out of the arcs of history, the tracing of historical cause and effect, the preservation of the memory of the past. The purpose of the work is not to deny reality but to affirm it, to affirm the particular reality of the world of Kiyomori and his heirs. And its mood of besetting sorrow springs from the fact that the inhabitants of that world, as well as the author himself, can never turn their eyes away from, can never forget, the past. It is a lament upon the burden of memory.

The statue of the lay priest Kiyomori likewise is an affirmation and painstaking embodiment of reality. Like the *Tale*, it dates from the early Kamakura era, and though the modeling is not so detailed as in some other portrait statues of that period, it is unmistakably a representation of a particular man engaged in a particular act. His long fingers curl about the scrolls as he holds them up to the light to get a better view. His head is inclined slightly to one side, his brow wrinkled, as though he was a little puzzled by the words he is reading. His face is not strikingly spiritual, nor yet sensual, but sedate and powerful, with a large nose, wide full lips, and crystal eyeballs that gleam in the spotlight from below. His head and shoulders cast long shadows across the gold screen at his back, while banners of green and gold and orange, hanging from the dark fretted ceiling, stir by his side in the wind.

During the Heian period, Japanese sculptors had seemed content to spend their time fashioning images of Buddhist deities—great Amidas and Yakushi Nyorais, beings of another world whose lives span countless eons, sitting in expressionless meditation, their eyes staring vacantly ahead. And then, in the Kamakura period, after the fall of the Heike, they suddenly began to make lifelike portraits of historical personages. Suddenly they turned from the ageless Buddhas and set about to capture and preserve the features and motions of ordinary human beings. Something must have happened to convince them that the accidents of time and place and existence—a man named Kiyomori, who lived in a house near here and died of a raging fever in 1181—were not meaningless phantoms after all.

It is one thing to go off and be other-worldly while the world is still comfortably in existence at one's elbow, but another matter again when it is the world itself that does the departing. And it was a world, the whole world of the Heian era, that departed with the Tairas from Kyoto. The Heike fled west to destruction, the center of political power shifted from Kyoto to Kamakura, and the Japanese found themselves abruptly deposited in the Middle Ages. If the experience impressed upon them the transience of earthly glory, it at the same time no doubt awakened in their minds a vivid longing for the past. This, perhaps, is the reason for their sudden and earnest desire, so obvious in the *Tale* and in this statue, to recall once more the color of a robe, the sound of a voice, the exact features of a face.

"I wonder if that's what Kiyomori really looked like?" I remarked to the priest.

"It is impossible to tell who made the statue," he replied, "or whether the artist ever actually saw Kiyomori. So I suppose no one will ever know. Anyway," he added, "if it doesn't look like Kiyomori, it at least looks like somebody!"

He was right. It certainly did look like somebody, and that, I reflected, was what mattered.

We had left the hall and were walking along a veranda at the side, when the priest suddenly pointed to the ground under the eaves. "That's Kiyomori's grave," he said, indicating a heap of weathered stones, colored a soft orange in the late afternoon sun.

1959

The Black Fudō

Osaka, the largest commercial city in Japan, consists of one extravagantly broad and beautiful avenue—Mido-suji—and mile on mile of factories and grubby little shops and houses, sprawled over a muddy coastal plain laced with rivers and sluggish gray canals. Since the war destroyed about three-fourths of the city, most of the houses are new—two-story frame and plaster boxes pushed up against each other, with narrow, stifling rooms and stairways so cramped you have to crawl up them on all fours, crowded to the bursting point with inhabitants. Nowhere is the press of overpopulation more apparent, nowhere does the flimsy postwar architecture seem in greater danger of being battered to pieces by the endless waves of humanity that surge merrily about it. You can see it wearing away before your eyes.

Perhaps because I live and work in Kyoto and go to Osaka only for recreation, I have a great fondness for the latter. Nothing is pleasanter, when the stuffy provincialism and over-inquisitive neighbors of Kyoto begin to wear one down, than to get on an express and glide off to the fresh air and bustle of the seacoast. I have even mentioned to Kyoto friends that I might try living in Osaka sometime, a suggestion that makes them blink with horror. On the subject of Osaka they recall that in the bombing raids it burned with a lovely red glow, lighting up the night sky. Otherwise they express only contempt for a city that, they say, devotes itself wholly to business. "*Shōbai, shōbai*—that's all they care about down there!" complain the high-

45

minded citizens of Kyoto, and snicker at the way Osakaites salute each other with the inquiry "Making any money?"

As in most Japanese cities, a considerable part of Osaka's *shōbai* consists in feeding, wining, and diverting itself. The principal entertainment center is in the south, between Shinsaibashi and Namba. Here are the kabuki and puppet theaters, the vaudeville houses and strip shows, the cheapest movies and the most expensive geisha. Here too are the thousands of restaurants, bars, and snack stands in which Osakaites, according to the proverbial expression, "eat themselves bankrupt."

In the center of this district is a tiny walled area of lanterns and shrines known as Hōzen-ji, all that remains of what was once a large temple. Hōzen-ji was formerly part of another temple, Chikurin-ji, built at the beginning of the Tokugawa period as a special place of worship for the members of the outcast class who lived in the area. From the *Sennichi-nembutsu,* or "Thousand Days Invocation of the Buddha's Name," which was performed there, it came to be known as Sennichi Temple, a designation that survives in place-names in the neighborhood.

Any of these names would have brought shudders to an Osakaite of the Tokugawa period. Though bordered by a row of theaters on the north, the district at that time was little more than one vast crematorium and graveyard, enlivened by an execution ground where the exposed heads of criminals grinned at passing citizens. They say that even today if you dig deep enough in the area you can turn up old bones, though I have had no opportunity to test the assertion.

At the beginning of the Meiji period the graveyard and crematorium were moved to Abeno, and Hōzen-ji and the other temples around, their chief source of income vanished, fell into decline. The teahouses nearby, however, which up until this time had done a modest business serving refreshments to grieving relatives, began to thrive, drawing crowds of pleasure-seekers who would not have ventured near the place in its creepier days. Among the voluminous *shōbai* lore of Osakaites is a saying that businesses built on the sites of graveyards always prosper. The case of the Hōzen-ji teahouses and restaurants seems to be good proof. Over the years they grew larger and more numerous until they had pushed their old patron, Hōzen-ji, into a little square of land in the middle. When the whole area was flattened in the bombing, Hōzen-ji suffered a final blow; all that is left of it now are a few small shrines in a courtyard of stone flags, a tiny vortex of faith in a sea of shimmering neon and glassy black canals.

At one side of the courtyard is the shrine of Kompira, an Indian deity honored as the guardian of ships and seamen, whose popularity seems secure in the port city of Osaka. Across from him is an even more popular deity, Fudō-myōō, the dispeller of demons and delusion. Carved in black stone, he stands in the open, holding a sword and glaring ferociously, backed by another stone, a thin oval cut in the shape of leaping flames. Before him are ranged pots of smoking incense and stone racks with votive candles. Worshippers with a request draw water from a well in the yard and throw it over him with dippers—not a gentle, etherealized aspersion such as one is subjected to at a High Mass, but great drenching splashes, with a dipperful for each of the little stone guardians who stand by his side, their heads bristling with damp green moss. Only then do the petitioners stand back, clap their hands and state their request. It is from this ritual that he takes his name, *Mizukake*, or "Water-splashed Fudō," though whether the purpose is to purify him, to relieve him from the heat of the flames that dance behind him, or merely to attract his attention, I have been unable to discover. Whatever the significance of the ritual, there would seem to be little reason to doubt its efficacy. Day and night a stream of worshippers pass before his shrine: smartly dressed geisha and mistresses of restaurants, maids and apprentices from the neighborhood, dousing and clapping, lighting candles and incense and petitioning for success in the great concern of Osaka life—*shōbai*. Swish with the water, clap-clap of the hands: May my business prosper! May my request be granted! *Onegai itashimasu, onegai itashimasu!* Then turn and patter off down the narrow stone alley, making way for the next petitioner.

I watched the worshippers one night dousing the black Fudō and bowing their heads, the court lit by red paper lanterns and countless dribbling candles, and stood in the shadows trying to catch what they were saying. After a while I began to feel conspicuous and ducked into a sushi stand by the edge of the shrine to have some sake and fresh squid.

On one side of me at the long counter were three young men, office workers on their way home, their heads in a huddle, drinking beer and discussing the stock market. On the other side a young girl sat up stiff and demure on her stool eating roasted mushrooms with her father and mother, while at the end two fat middle-aged businessmen wiped their faces with hot towels. The proprietor and a young apprentice bustled behind the counter, heating sake and worrying bits of seafood into appetizing shapes.

"What will you have?" the proprietor asked the fat merchants. They peered thoughtfully at the glass case of raw fish on ice in front of them.

"What's good?"

"The tuna's good. But rather high."

They nodded for him to fix some. "How high?"

"About fifteen hundred yen a hundred *momme*."

"*Heeh*," they wheezed. "That high?"

"This piece is worth around three thousand yen!" the proprietor said proudly, holding up a small cube of the pink, fat-streaked flesh from the belly of the tuna in the palm of his hand.

The merchants picked up the pieces of tuna sushi he had fixed for them and with slow, appreciative fingers, dipped them in the soy sauce and laid them gently in their mouths as though they were depositing gold nuggets in a safe. "So high!" they murmured, swallowing with a look of profound satisfaction.

After a while the prim young lady and her parents paid their bill and left—a well-timed exit, as it turned out.

They had not been gone long when the door rattled open a little on its rollers and a woman's face peered in from the darkness, giggling. "I look a mess! Do you suppose it's all right if I come in?"

It was an odd way to make an entrance and I looked at the proprietor to see what it might mean. But he only glanced nervously at the apprentice and the two of them bent over their preparations, suddenly very busy.

The door opened all the way and the woman stepped in. She was heavily made up and wore a white, summery kimono with splashy flower designs. She rolled the door shut behind her and swooped down the length of the counter to where the merchants sat. "Excuse me! Excuse me!" She pushed her way along, clutching several small boxes to her breast.

"Good evening, gentlemen! How would you like to buy some of these?" She held out a box. I was too far away to make out the label.

The merchants looked up with heavy, expressionless faces. "What are they?" one of them asked.

The young men beside me stopped talking and watched the woman. She giggled and flounced her shoulders. "I can't *explain* what they are," she shrilled. "But I'll bet you can guess!" She flourished the box over her head and shook it seductively. It rattled as though it were full of walnuts.

"I have no idea," said the man, turning away.

For a moment she wavered, as if she would give the whole thing up and leave. Then she pulled herself together and began to pout. "Now don't get angry. Here, I'll let you have a peek." She put the box on the counter and opened the lid a little way. "All different kinds for all different uses. But you mustn't ask me to explain or I'd be too embarrassed!"

She gave his shoulder a playful shove and he smiled faintly, showing his gold teeth.

"You speak with a Kyushu accent—is that where you're from?" he inquired, gravely changing the subject.

"Oh no, I'm from Osaka. But I think a Kyushu accent goes better with this line of work. That's where they make these, you know"—clattering the box again. "Kyushu people are so passionate and . . ."

I wondered if there wasn't some way she could peddle her goods without all these leers and gushes, though it was hard to imagine any other approach.

"I'll give you a hundred yen for the boxful," the man said, opening his eyes wider to watch the effect of this. One eye slanted up at a sharper angle than the other, giving his face a lopsided look like that of the kabuki actor Ganjirō.

"You're joking!" She laughed uneasily. "They cost four hundred a box to begin with and I have to get them all the way from Kyushu. And if the police catch me . . ."

"A hundred yen, no more."

"A hundred yen for *one*, maybe, but not the whole box. Here, let me show you what you can *do* with them." She took the top of the box off. The young men on the other side of me looked away and reached for their beer. "Now this one is for when you . . ."

But the man only stared at her with cold, half-closed eyes. All her giggling and shrilling, the theatrical, whiny voice that was meant to sound suggestive, summoned no other response than sullen indifference.

Which was odd. No one in the room at the time could conceivably have been shocked at the appearance of a woman peddling sex gadgets. Sex is treated rather openly in Japan and, next to illness, is perhaps the favorite topic of conversation in moments of relaxation. Geisha—described somewhat vaguely in Western guide books as "witty conversationalists"—make their living by talking amusingly about it, as do their less costly counterparts, bar girls and the proprietresses of sake stands. Indeed few people in the eating and drinking business in Japan seem to find it necessary or expedient to talk of much else with their customers, except a few intellectually inclined bar madams who cater to students and specialize in discussing foreign movies instead.

But whether it is a geisha, a bar girl, or a sake-stand proprietress, the participation of a woman is imperative for the success of any such conversation. All-male "bull sessions" on the subject, so popular in more puritanical countries like America, are regarded in Japan as rather pointless, if not actually in bad taste.

The arrival of the woman peddler in the sushi shop, therefore, might well have provided the necessary complement for such a discussion, sparking an animated exchange of jokes and laughter. The merchants would take up one of her remarks and begin to weave a fabric of puns and double-entendres, the favorite form of Japanese humor, crinkling their eyes at her while she protested her embarrassment in elaborate squeals, and before long the proprietor and his apprentice would join in, for fun and because it was good for business, and the young men beside me would slap the counter and guffaw.

But this woman was trying too hard, flapping and flouncing like an earnest white bird. She was not there to provide amusing conversation, like a geisha or a bar girl, but to sell expensive and questionable wares which no one wanted. The evening was too young, the group too sober still, and the fat merchant refused to take up her innuendoes for fear she would mistake his response for a desire to buy. Instead he had evidently decided to tease her by haggling over price.

"A hundred yen," he repeated perversely.

"You're awful!" she screeched, swinging her arm around to give him another push. He pulled back in time and her long white sleeve, like a fluttering wing, caught the box and knocked it off the counter. The contents skittered over the muddy floor.

"Sorry," said the man.

"Never mind. It was my fault," she said softly as she bent to pick them up. If she was annoyed, she didn't let it show. "Some of them got kind of dirty," she reported, smiling up at him. "I guess I'll have to let you have the box for a hundred yen after all."

The man wheeled around quickly and faced the counter. "Is that order of sushi ready to take out yet? I promised my wife I'd bring her home some." His voice was all virtuous concern.

"In a minute," said the proprietor, raising his head for the first time since the woman entered. There was a short silence.

"Well?" said the woman, standing quite still by the man's side.

"Well what?"

"Aren't you going to buy them?"

"I don't want any!" He fluttered his chubby hand in impatient refusal, looking the other way. *"Iran! Iran!"*

"Not even for a hundred yen?"

"Iran-te!"

"Your Honor might have been so kind as to inform me of that in the first place!" She took advantage of the choicest honorifics to make her anger quite clear. Then she gathered up her things and rolled open the door. "Sorry to have bothered you," she said, smiling and nodding to the rest of us from the doorway.

The thick-lidded, gold-teethed merchants turned with a look of defiance and watched her go out. Then they swung back to the counter and began muttering together.

I paid my check and wandered out into the courtyard, feeling vaguely depressed. The woman was there, drawing a pail of water from the well. She carried it briskly across the court and set it down with a bang beside one of the stone lanterns. I could see her boxes stacked neatly on the base of the lantern. Then she took a dipper and began scooping up the water and dashing it over the black Fudō. As I turned and walked down the alley I heard the sound of her energetic sloshing, followed by the crisp, resounding clap of her hands. Her approach to the deity was brusque and matter-of-fact, with a hint of impatience, as though she were reprimanding a lazy business partner. *"Onegai itashimasu!"* For what it might be worth, I seconded her petition.

1960

Green Valley

I first saw the village of Aoya—Green Valley—from the train going to Matsue. I was thinking of stopping somewhere along the Japan Sea coast to swim for a few days on my way back from Matsue to Kyoto, and I noticed that, on the map of Tottori Prefecture spread out on my lap, Aoya, a little west of Tottori City, was marked with the small red flag that indicated a bathing beach. I asked the young man in the seat next to me if he knew anything about the place, but he said he had never gotten off the train there. He was from Matsue, he told me, but had been working for the past three years in Tokyo. He was immaculately dressed in a new suit and held a transistor radio clamped intently to his ear all the time we were talking—evidently an important symbol of his success in the Eastern Capital.

I asked about places to see in Matsue, but he was not very helpful and volunteered the opinion that I would probably find it a very dull town. As the train pulled into the station, a woman's shrill voice came over the loudspeaker in the car. "We are now entering the city of Matsue. Situated on beautiful Lake Shinji and threaded with canals, it is often called the Venice of the East." The young man glanced at me with an embarrassed frown. "I don't know why they have to say silly things like that," he said.

After two days in Matsue, I took a local train going back east and, though I still knew nothing about the place, got off at Aoya. The green valley of its name was formed by a small river that wound between two hills and emptied into a broad, sluggish estuary. Following what seemed to be the main street, I walked in the hot midday sun from the sta-

54

tion right through the narrow, dusty village and out onto the beach, but saw no sign of an inn. I was beginning to wonder if I would have to give up and go back to the station, when I found a policeman who pointed out an inn that backed on the estuary just off the main road.

After the usual conversation with the proprietress— Yes, I can sleep on a futon; no, I don't have to have steak for dinner—she took me to a room on the second floor overlooking the river. I left my things, changed into my bathing suit and went back to the beach.

It was a beautiful beach, broad, with fine white sand, and deserted except for some boys playing in the water around the diving platform. I swam out to the platform, sunbathed a while, and listened to their conversation, very little of which I could follow. Partly this was due to the fact that I wasn't on to the local dialect yet, though Japanese schoolboys as a rule talk so fast and chew up their words so that I can seldom understand them no matter what dialect they are speaking.

I returned to my room at sundown. The heat of the day had broken and the river was dark green and looked very deep, although here and there you could see streamers of sea grass waving languidly in the current just below the surface. A boy was swimming alone in the middle, not for pleasure, obviously, but for training, making long, slow, purposeful journeys upstream and then resting while the current carried him back down toward the sea, the rhythmical splash of his arms the only sound that broke the silence of the twilight.

The next morning I spent swimming from a cape that jutted out into the ocean east of the beach. I had gotten there by a road that ran up over one of the hills, but I decided to try to go back along the shore, though this involved climbing over or swimming around a number of rocky points. As I rounded one of these, I suddenly came on a large party of men, women, and children picnicking on a wooden platform built over the rocks. A tin roof shielded them from the burning sun. In the cove nearby several women were diving for shellfish, disappearing under the waves for impossibly long intervals and surfacing with the thin, mournful whistle that divers make when they expel their breath. The shells they had gathered they plunked into wooden tubs that bobbed in the water beside them.

I stood watching the diving women and trying to look as hungry as possible, which was not difficult, considering it was after one and I had had no lunch. After a long and clearly audible discussion among the picnickers as to what language to address me in—the conclusion being that, since no one spoke English, there was really no choice—I was hailed in Japanese and invited to join the group. The women passed around plates of raw fish and squid, boiled octopus in vinegar, cucumber and eggplant pickles, cold watermelon, and the big, tasty *hotategai,* or crusader's scallops, that are a specialty of this region, while the men poured me beer, sake, port wine, and whisky and informed me that, since I had come late, I would have to drink very fast to catch up. Everyone wanted to know how I had happened to come to Aoya—nobody ever did, they said—and kept insisting I must have gotten off the train by mistake.

At first I had taken them for fishermen, but it turned out that they all worked at a dairy and were having their annual outing. The man who had hailed me, and who seemed to be in charge of the party, presented me with his card, which said that his name was Nishikawa and he was an expert in artificial insemination. Since I had nothing to say on that subject, I asked him about Aoya, and in the course of the conversation discovered one thing that had been troubling me about the local dialect.

People in the Kyoto area often use *ke* instead of the standard *ka* for the interrogative particle that is attached to the end of a sentence to make everything that goes before into a question. I had assumed that the final *ke* which I kept hearing in Aoya was this same interrogative, and this was leading to all sorts of mysterious exchanges such as the following:

I: Is it all right to swim from those rocks?

Aoyaite: No. Is it deep?

I (somewhat confused): What if it is deep?

Aoyaite: Are there likely to be sharks?

The solution to this muddle, which I pass along for anyone who may happen to visit Tottori, is that the final *ke* is not an interrogative at all but, like the final *ken* in dialects farther to the west, means "because" and is used at the ends of sentences which explain the reason for something. Once this realization dawned on me, I found the speech of the Aoyaites considerably less enigmatic.

After we had eaten and drunk a great deal and the smaller children had had time for a short nap, Mr. Nishikawa announced that we would all visit the lighthouse on the end of the cape. We piled into two engine-powered open boats and set off, bouncing wildly over the swells that pounded in over the rocks. There had been a lot to drink and no one seemed to be very familiar with the handling of small boats, so that the voyage had a delightfully daring and abandoned air. Men sang songs and shouted for the boats to go faster, wives rashly stood up and nearly fell overboard, children screamed, engines sputtered and stalled—it was a lively expedition indeed.

After some time, we arrived at the base of an escarpment and, with intensified shouting and squealing, scrambled out of the boats and filed up a steep trail that wound back and forth across the face of the escarpment.

Up in the lighthouse we all signed our names in the guest book and looked at the ocean through a telescope (it was too hazy to see Oki, the only offshore island in the area). Three people talking at once tried to explain to me some legend connected with this part of the coast about a rabbit and a school of sharks. On the way back to the boats, Mr. Nishikawa asked if I was married, and when I said I wasn't, he offered to arrange things with his younger sister, who was walking just behind us. She screeched with laughter and gave him such a shove I thought he would go head first down the cliff. A friend was commissioned to take a picture of the three of us—the last exposure on the roll—which was immediately discovered to have been ruined because no one had remembered to wind the film.

That night, shortly after dinner, the maid came to my room to say there was someone on the phone for me. It was Mr. Nishikawa, reporting that the party was continuing at a drinking stand near the station and inviting me to come. He said there was a festival at the village shrine and we would all go over to it later in the evening.

When I got there, I found him and a friend from the dairy drinking sake. His wife and sister had gone on home, but his little boy was sitting beside him at the counter drinking a bottle of milk. After a while we left and went to a restaurant nearby. We were shown to a room upstairs and were joined by two girls in kimonos bringing sake, beer, and more of the big scallops.

One of the girls spoke a few words of English, which she said she had learned working in a bar in Okayama. She was husky and dark-complexioned and had a loud voice. From the way Mr. Nishikawa teased and joked with her, it was obvious they were old friends.

The other girl, as though for contrast, was pale and demure. Unlike her companion, she took very little of the sake or beer offered her, and soon got herself deeply involved teaching me the words to a popular song about a hawk circling in the evening sky. Mr. Nishikawa's son had a bottle of orange pop and promptly fell asleep, while his father drank with the big dark girl. They were having a contest to see who could down a glass of beer faster, and with each try her voice got louder and more surly. Then she began to swear.

There is an odd notion among many foreigners that the Japanese language has no swear words. This comes about, I think, because they try to find exact equivalents in Japanese for European swear words, only to discover that these either don't exist or, if they do, are not considered nearly so shocking. This leads them to believe that people in Japan never cuss at each other—a wholly erroneous conclusion and one which, considering how excitable and loquacious the Japanese can be on occasion, they should know is extremely unlikely.

Languages like English or Chinese achieve a scurrilous effect by the addition of epithets or expletives that serve to suggest all sorts of awful things about the parentage or moral habits of the person addressed. Japanese, on the other hand, gets the same effect by purely formal means. Just as there is an elaborate set of honorific pronouns, verbs, and verb endings which are used to express varying degrees of respect when speaking to or about others, so there is a complementary set for expressing varying degrees of contempt. The sting of the latter comes not from any scurrility explicit in the words themselves, but from the insulting implication of inferior social status that they carry. (While most textbooks of Japanese explain the honorifics of the language in the first few lessons, none, so far as I know, lists the pejoratives. This is probably just as well, since words that carry such a high emotional charge can be dangerous in the hands of beginners, and I seriously warn readers not to play around with the examples that follow unless they are prepared to talk their way out of the misunderstandings that will result.)

Up to this point, Mr. Nishikawa's lady companion had been using ordinary polite language to him. Now, as she got drunker and more irritated at his teasing, she shifted gears and started down into the basement.

He was betting her she couldn't drink a whole container of sake at one gulp.

"Nani nukasu ka!"—"What are you talking about?" (first degree of contempt), she said, and proceeded to execute the feat. The other girl laughed nervously and hastily began explaining to me the words of the second verse of the hawk song.

"You got it down all right," conceded Mr. Nishikawa. "But I'll bet it'll all come back up in a minute—just like the last time!"

"Nani nukashi yagaru!"—"What are you talking about?" (second degree of contempt), said the girl, glowering at him. We all sat silent while she snatched another container of sake from the table and downed it in one gulp too. She wobbled dizzily as she held the container over her head and shook out the last drop.

Mr. Nishikawa, obviously not one to recognize enough of a good thing when he saw it, grinned at her sardonically. "I wouldn't use language like that if I couldn't hold my sake any better than you!" he said.

"Nani nukashite ketsukaru!"—"What are you talking about?" (third degree of contempt), she blurted out thickly. Having thus scraped the bottom of the linguistic barrel, she lunged at him in dumb fury, but he dodged and she hit her head with a loud bang on the pillar of the tokonoma. Groaning softly, she sank to the floor of the tokonoma and then, as Mr. Nishikawa had predicted, got sick, throwing up all over the flower arrangement.

After that she felt much better and, when the mess had been cleaned up, Mr. Nishikawa got her to her feet and we all started off for the shrine. She was still very drunk and fell down several times on the way, but we managed to get to the shrine before the last of the festivities were over.

The next morning when I packed my bag and brought it down to the entrance of the inn, I found a high school student in a neatly pressed uniform standing in the doorway. He bowed politely, said he had heard I was staying at the inn, and asked if I would please tell him all about America. I said I had to catch a train, but assured him that if I could manage it I would come back to Aoya the following summer and explain things to him then.

1961

Michizane and the Plums

The tree known as the Japanese apricot, to begin with an anomaly, is native to China, not Japan, its small white flowers being a favorite subject of Chinese painters and poets; its Latin name is *Prunus mume*, from *mume* or *ume*, the Japanese version of the Chinese name *mei*; and practically everyone outside of horticultural experts refers to it in English as a plum. If all of that is quite clear, I will add that it is revered in China and Japan as a symbol of fortitude because it blooms in winter, before any other flower will venture out. In Kyoto, this means February, and as far as I am concerned, it means fortitude, at least for any living thing that feels about the Kyoto winter as I do.

The customary place in Kyoto to view plum flowers is in the grounds of the Kitano Tenjin Shrine, situated in the northwest sector of the old city. The main building of the present shrine was built some three and a half centuries ago and is in the florid style typical of late Momoyama architecture. Beautiful as it is, with its intricate roofs and splashes of red and gold, it conveys a somewhat false impression of the antiquity of the shrine, which is actually much older, dating from the middle of the tenth century. Clustered around the main building is an assortment of smaller shrines, monuments, and stone lanterns of all shapes, and among these grow the flowering plums for which the shrine is famous. Small trees, alarmingly bent and hollowed, they give the impression of having been subjected to almost intolerable buffeting and strain, which is why, when their scattering of delicate white flowers emerges each year from the blackened trunks to face the cold, they present such a poignant symbol of a modest but dogged determination to go on living. The plums are planted there in honor of the patron deity of the shrine, Kitano Tenjin, because they were his favorite flower.

Kitano Tenjin was not always a god. He was born in 845 as Sugawara no Michizane, the third son of a court scholar in the Kyoto of the early Heian period. Exceptionally bright and diligent, he in time became a scholar-official himself and won renown for his skill in writing Chinese verse and prose.

Chinese studies, encouraged by a succession of erudite emperors, were only slightly past the height of their popularity. Japanese envoys and monks journeyed to the mainland, Chinese merchants came to Kyoto, and Classical Chinese was the language used for all state or learned papers. Officials were chosen from among candidates who had passed examinations in Chinese studies modeled after those of the T'ang bureaucratic system, and government and private schools in the capital, staffed by men like Michizane's father, tutored the sons of the aristocracy in the reading and composition of Chinese poetry and prose.

Michizane surpassed all of the other men of his time in composing Chinese verse, which is to say that he was able to go beyond the stereotyped themes and sentiments expected of a court scholar—"Farewell to the Envoy from Pohai," "Viewing Chrysanthemums at an Official Banquet," etc.—and to use the medium to depict the actual scenes around him and the emotions they evoked. In one poem, for example, written in the early part of his life, he describes the ruins of a Kyoto mansion that had burned the year before, with its bright tiles strewn in the ashes, its half-charred pine tree, its ornamental lake with the little island where only rats live now. In another, on the death of his little son, he lists the things that remind him of the dead child:

Your mulberry bow over the door, the mugwort
  arrows;
your stilts by the hedge top, the riding whip of vine;
in the garden the flower seeds we planted in fun;
on the wall, the words you'd learned, your scribblings
  beside them—

Or, writing in a lighter vein, he describes setting off for
work early in the morning through the snowy streets of
Kyoto to the palace, wrapped in a fur robe and fortified
with a drink of hot sake. I am reminded of the winter
mornings when I used to travel much the same route on
my way to teach an early class at Dōshisha University—
warmed, I might add, by neither of Michizane's comforts.

Like his father, Michizane became a distinguished
teacher, and his poetic works contain an interesting series
of poems written in 883 to congratulate ten of his students
on passing the state examination, in which he praises the
younger ones for their precocity, and comforts the older
ones—one man had apparently been trying most of his life
to pass—with the reminder that, in Lao Tzu's words,
"great vessels are a long time in the making." His students
by custom remained loyal to their teacher and his interests
after they entered government service, and for this reason
Michizane and his clique soon came to pose a serious
threat to the power of the Fujiwara family, who dominated
the court and maintained a school of their own. It is not
surprising to find, therefore, that in 886 Michizane was ap-
pointed governor of the province of Sanuki, in northeast
Shikoku, and dispatched from the capital.

Michizane no doubt regretted leaving the cultured society of Kyoto, though he seems to have done his best to be
a conscientious provincial administrator. Interestingly, he
did not, like so many Heian aristocrats, complain of the
crude and uncouth ways of the country, at least in his po-

etry. Instead, in the best humanist tradition of the great T'ang poets, he composed a series of poems on the hardships of the people. Beginning with the refrain "Who does the cold come early to?" and employing the same rhymes throughout, the poems describe in succinct detail the bitter lot of the runaway peasant, the wandering beggar, the widower, the orphan, the herb gardener, the post-station attendant, the ferryman, the salt peddler, the fisherman, and the wood gatherer.

Back in the capital in 890, he rose rapidly in office and imperial favor, and in 894 was accorded the highest recognition as a scholar of Chinese by being chosen to head a diplomatic mission to the T'ang court. Surprisingly enough, after receiving the appointment, he almost immediately submitted a memorial advising the suspension of all such missions to the Chinese mainland. As with so many of Michizane's actions, we can only guess at his true motives. His apologists claim that, for all his Chinese learning, he realized that Japan no longer needed to seek leadership or cultural guidance from the continent; his detractors, on the other hand, suggest that he did not, for private political reasons, wish to absent himself from the capital, or that he suddenly lost his nerve at the prospect of the perilous sea journey. No one denies that travel to and in China at this time was dangerous, and that the political situation on the continent was highly unsettled— the T'ang dynasty collapsed eleven years later. It is quite possible, therefore, that Michizane acted neither out of fear nor scheming ambition when he suggested that a dangerous, expensive, and questionable diplomatic mission be canceled. In any event, the mission was called off and he never got to China; like the great Japanese sinologues of the Tokugawa era, he died without ever having visited the country whose literature and language he spent a lifetime studying.

Michizane continued to rise in power until, by 899, he held the second highest post in the government, that of Udaijin, or Minister of the Right. This was a dangerous height, one which his rivals at court could no longer tolerate. In 901 he was abruptly accused of various treasonable acts and ordered into exile at the Dazaifu in northern Kyushu. We will never know the real facts of the case, since nearly all the documents pertaining to it were deliberately destroyed shortly after his death. But certain circumstances surrounding the move, including the fact that the emperor's father, the Retired Emperor Uda, under whom Michizane had served with distinction, was prevented from appealing on his behalf or even examining the charges, suggest that they were dubious at best. Michizane's wife and most of his numerous children were forced to remain in the capital or were exiled elsewhere. Only the youngest son and daughter, still in their childhood, were permitted to accompany their father.

Life at the Dazaifu in Kyushu would have been hard even for a man not accustomed to the comforts of the capital. The official lodging assigned to Michizane was a shambles—the roof leaked, the floor was rotten, the verandas had fallen in. He suffered from beriberi and stomach trouble, for which his wife sent him medicine from the capital when she could, and the loneliness of exile was deepened by the death of his little son shortly after his arrival. The poems which he wrote during this period, naturally enough, are full of grief and longing: he receives with sadness the news of the death of a friend in the capital, he recalls the honors he had enjoyed in the past, he worries about what the Kyoto snow is doing to his favorite bamboos. Gradually malnutrition weakened him to the point where he could hardly walk. A poem written in 902 and entitled "The Lamp Goes Out" conveys with great subtlety the state of his mind at this time:

It was not the wind—the oil is gone;
I hate the lamp that will not see me through
    the night.
How hard—to make ashes of the mind, to still
    the body!
I rise and move into the moonlight by the cold
    window.

It was too much to expect that Michizane could, in Chuang Tzu's phrase, "make the mind like dead ashes," for the events of the past still weighed too heavily upon him. But though he could not rise above feeling, he could restrain it; like the devout Buddhist that he was, he speaks, in these last poems, in sorrow, but never in anger or resentment. He died early in 903, having watched the plums blossom one last time.

Death, and the circumstances under which it comes, can do strange things to a man's reputation. Not many years after Michizane passed away in Kyushu, a series of disasters fell upon the capital—persistent drought and plague, the premature death of several of Michizane's old rivals of the Fujiwara family, the death of two crown princes in succession. To the men of the time, it seemed obvious that the angry spirit of Michizane was exacting its revenge, and steps were hurriedly taken to appease it. Michizane was restored to his former position and title and accorded other posthumous honors, and when these moves failed to put an end to the strange happenings, a shrine was set up in the area called Kitano, or North Field, where offerings were made to him under the title Temmangū Tenjin. This is the origin of the present Kitano Tenjin Shrine.

It is ironic that the mild and bookish Michizane should have been worshipped first as a god of wrath and vengeance. But fear of the supernatural was a very real part of

Heian life, and the men of the time believed that an unjust death could work terrible changes in the soul. It was not long, however, before the memories of Michizane's distinguished career, rather than of his tragic end, began to dominate the popular conception of the god Tenjin. In time, the man who had lectured on Chinese historical texts, written a learned preface to a treatise on Buddhism by the famous monk Ennin, compiled works on Japanese history, and won acclaim for his poetry in Japanese and Chinese, became recognized as the patron deity of literature and learning. At a much later date, he also came to be revered as the god of calligraphy, though there is no historical evidence to indicate that he ever excelled in that art. Perhaps the strangest cult associated with his name is that which arose among the Zen monks of the Muromachi period who, like Michizane, were enthusiastic students and writers of Chinese verse and who favored a synthesis of Buddhist, Confucian, and Taoist doctrines. They declared that he had in fact visited China, and there studied Zen under a master of the Sung dynasty—founded half a century after his death. They even produced pictures of him as he appeared in dreams, wearing the cap of a Taoist immortal, the robes of a Zen monk, and carrying a branch of the ubiquitous plum.

The plum was to Michizane what the cherry has been to so many of his countrymen—a symbol of spring which is at the same time a reminder of the swift passing of time—and he wrote of it most often in a mood of gentle sorrow. His most famous poem on the subject is the one in Japanese which he composed early in 901 as he was taking leave of his family, his friends, and the plum trees in his garden, before going into exile:

When east winds blow,
send out your fragrance,
plum flowers—
though masterless,
do not forget the spring!

In 902, the year before his death, he wrote one of his last poems on the subject, this one in Chinese, in which he recalls the times he had composed poems to the plums in the garden of his house in Sempū Ward in Kyoto, or at the banquets in the imperial palace:

The ones newly planted north of Sempū Ward,
the ones at banquet time west of Jijū Palace:
different plums, though the same man sang
   to them—
how the flowers must have laughed at all my
   grieving!

Michizane wrote in a literary tradition that condoned the expression of sorrow, indeed made it the chief theme of poetry, and his poems, like those of his contemporaries in China and Japan, are dominated by a mood of melancholy. But he showed true genius, it seems to me, when, though ill, lonely, and in exile, he somehow managed just before his death to transcend the tradition and his own sorrow, and to look at himself for once from the point of view of the plums. "How the flowers must have laughed . . ."

1964

Doburoku Days

I have been asked to write something about my life as a teacher and graduate student in Japan. My experiences were in some ways rather special, and are by now probably hopelessly out of date, but for what they may be worth, I outline them below.

I went to Japan in August of 1951, using the last of my GI savings to get there. I had completed an M.A. in Chinese studies at Columbia that year but was no longer registered as a graduate student and had no definite plans for a Ph.D. There were few grants or fellowships in those days, and fewer prospects for jobs, but through the help of Japanese friends, I managed to secure two positions in Japan, one as an English teacher at Doshisha University in Kyoto, the other as a research assistant to Professor Yoshikawa Kōjirō of the Chinese Language and Literature Department of Kyoto University. The Occupation was in force, food was still rather scarce, and there were very few Americans in Japan other than missionaries or those connected with the military. Professor Yoshikawa, who acted as my guarantor, was advised by colleagues (I later learned) that he was taking a fearful risk by inviting me to work under him, since "foreigners must be fed large quantities of meat each day or they will sicken and die." Fortunately, Yoshikawa decided to be daring, I arrived to assume my duties, and it was some years before I learned why he sometimes scrutinized me with such an apprehensive expression.

Because of my arrangement with Doshisha and Kyoto universities, I proved to have several advantages over students who arrived later on Ford or Fulbright grants. Though Doshisha offered to let me teach as many hours as I wished, I decided to keep to six hours a week so as to have as much time as possible for the study of Japanese (I had had only one year of the language before arriving in Japan). The combined salary from my two jobs, plus a few evenings of private tutoring a week in English, was about 18,000 yen, or $50, a month. This was not a great deal more than the average Japanese student had at his disposal, and meant that, even if I had not wished to, I was obliged to learn very quickly to live Japanese style. This had its grim side, particularly at first before I had become accustomed to Japanese food, but it made things infinitely easier in the years that followed. Also there was not much to buy in those days even if one had the money, and one could live, eat, and drink on sums that now seem incredible. For example, 150 yen got you a large tea kettle of *doburoku* (milky, unrefined rice wine), 50 yen a plate of assorted cow innards to be roasted at the table, and this provided a splendid evening's carousal for four. True, one paid a certain penalty the morning after, but that didn't seem to matter so much in those days.

My jobs at Doshisha and under Professor Yoshikawa gave me a definite "place" in Japanese society, such as no foreigner coming to the country simply as a graduate student could hope to have. As a teacher I enjoyed the courtesy and respect that that position commands, or at least used to command, in Japanese society. At Kyoto University I was treated the same as Professor Yoshikawa's other graduate students; at his recommendation, I made application to the university and was accepted as an "old system" student in the Department of Chinese Language and Literature. The "old system" led to no degree and required only a yearly report on the progress of one's research. It was abolished several years later and replaced with the

"new system" modeled on U.S. graduate school proce-
dures. Both my Doshisha and Kyoto University jobs required long hours of work, often spent in pursuits hardly,
if at all, related to East Asian studies, but they allowed me
to make friends and establish relationships that were of
great use later, and that would have been very hard to ac-
complish had I come merely as a student seeking to pursue
my own research.

I was particularly fortunate in being able to work under
Professor Yoshikawa, though I was as uncertain of what
the arrangement would lead to when I first entered into it
as he was. Among Japanese sinologists he has always been
noted for the interest he takes in Western sinological studies, and when, on my arrival, he discovered that I could
barely converse in either Chinese or Japanese, he gra-
ciously announced that he would take this opportunity to
improve his English conversation. The Chinese Language
and Literature Department was a small, convivial group,
given to parties, picnics, and drinking bouts at the slightest excuse, and much envied by other departments of
Kyoto University for the warm relations that existed between its faculty and students.

Finally, as a foreigner studying what is a foreign literature to the Japanese as well, I was spared that combination
of gross flattery ("Oh, you read characters much better
than we do!") and condescension ("After all, how can one
who is not a native ever hope to understand!") that plagues
Westerners studying Japanese literature in Japan or
Chinese literature in China. And because my specialty
was Chinese rather than Japanese, I felt free to enjoy those
things that interested me in Japanese culture such as the
Noh or kabuki theaters without constantly worrying
about how correctly or thoroughly I understood them,
while at the same time cavalierly ignoring things like the
tea ceremony that struck me as rather silly. This arrange-

ment, pleasant as it was, however, had one disadvantage—
a very serious one in my case. So congenial did I find life
in Japan that I never felt inclined to venture elsewhere and
so never learned to speak Chinese, the language that I was
supposed to be specializing in. This is the reason why,
though I doubt I would do any differently today, I always
caution my own graduate students not to follow my example.

Though I became a graduate student at Kyoto University in 1951, I attended very few classes for the first two
years. My knowledge of spoken Japanese allowed me to get
almost nothing out of lectures, and I found it unbearably
depressing to sit through two hours of unintelligible
drone. Moreover, since classrooms were unheated in those
days, and students were expected to remove their over-
coats if the professor removed his (he always did), a two-
hour lecture in the Kyoto winter could be a trial on more
than just linguistic grounds.

I did not enjoy teaching English conversation and always felt that I did it badly, so I was greatly relieved when
a stipend from Columbia for work on *Sources of Chinese
Tradition*, a textbook on Chinese intellectual history, allowed me to quit my Doshisha job at the end of the school
year in 1952. A Ford fellowship later in the year made it
possible to give up all my part-time jobs if I had so desired,
but I found my association with Professor Yoshikawa so
profitable to my studies that I gladly continued as his research assistant for several more years. I suppose it was
technically against the rules of the Ford grant to do so, but
it was of more value to me than most of the formal training
I received in Japanese universities.

Nowadays, like all responsible professors, I urge my students to push ahead with their research and finish up their
degrees, but I can't help wishing they wouldn't listen to
my advice so religiously, that they would show more in-

clination for dabbling in part-time jobs when they are in the East. Perhaps, if fellowship funds dry up, they will have to develop the inclination. By taking a job—any job—and performing some service for the people of the country, you show that you aren't there solely for the purpose of picking their brains, and you establish the kind of give-and-take relationship that is so vital if one is to get anything done in East Asian countries. Like many other Americans in Japan, I have in my time done huge quantities of translation, of everything from shirt advertisements and coffeehouse menus to medical reports on brain surgery and pamphlets for newfangled religions. Only once, when a rather wild-eyed man appeared at my lodgings with what he described as "an entirely new theory of the universe" which he wanted put into English, do I recall giving a flat refusal. Much of this translation work I did because I could not gracefully get out of it; much I did purely for the pay. But whatever the reason or the content of the material, I am convinced that it helped me enormously both in learning Japanese and in becoming a better translator. Translating is much like playing the piano: the more hours you spend at the keyboard, the better you get to be at it. If graduate students only could, or would, spend more time at such hack work, they would find that, when they come to tackle some really worthwhile and important text, they are much more likely to have the skill and facility to do it justice.

Since the above remarks may seem both dated and rather special in application, I will conclude with two words of general advice for Western students based on my twelve years of residence in Japan.

First, it's all right to "go" native, but don't ever succumb to the illusion that you can become one. Naturally, one ought to make every effort to adjust to the food, customs, and living conditions of the country he is visiting. The

Westerner who absolutely has to have a sandwich for lunch when there are nothing but rice and noodle dishes for miles in all directions is a burden to himself and a bore to everyone around. A sincere effort to use proper honorific forms of speech, to follow Oriental rules of etiquette, will be much appreciated, but remember always that it is the effort, and the impulse behind it, that is being appreciated, not the results. Americans, racially and ethnically a heterogeneous people, tend to think that nationality is largely a matter of language and custom, and that one will cease to be a foreigner when one adopts those of the country where one is residing. Needless to say, this is not the view of Asians. You may suppose that you are being as Japanese as the Japanese, that you have blended perfectly into the landscape, but there will always be someone at hand to exclaim on your amazing skill in using chopsticks and thereby remind you that in fact you are just as much a foreigner as the day you arrived. It is fun to write your name in characters and your Chinese or Japanese friends will encourage you to do so. But such a name, far from making you look like a native, by its very uncouthness loudly and unceasingly proclaims you to be an outsider, and in time you will probably prefer to return to a plain old signature.

Moreover, it is well to keep in mind that, while you are trying to follow Eastern ways, those about you may, out of courtesy, be trying to treat you according to their conception of Western ones. This can lead to much confusion and awkwardness—you bowing while your Japanese host sticks out his hand—but try to keep a sense of humor and do not let the occasion turn into a battle of wills.

Second—and this may seem to contradict what I have said above—beware your fellow countrymen. I do not mean by this that you should imitate those tiresome people who insist upon associating only with natives and boast that they haven't spoken a word of English in the past three months. On the contrary, especially during the early stages of your language study, you will find you need frequent opportunities to carry on rapid and sparkling conversations with fellow English-speakers just to convince yourself that you are not really the thick-tongued moron you appear to be when you attempt to speak Chinese or Japanese. I merely mean that, as a foreigner abroad, you are likely to come into contact with a wide variety of Westerners, some with interests and ways of life very different from yours, and this can lead to problems in socializing. What an American businessman on an expense account describes as a "very reasonable" restaurant may turn out to cost you half a month's rent, and a look at the kind of housing that such businessmen or diplomatic people can afford may send you back to your own shabby lodgings in a mood of deep discontent. For your own peace of mind, therefore, you may find it best to associate mainly with other academic people, whose interests in the country and financial means are approximately the same as yours.

Finally, above all be wary of casual acquaintances or friends-of-a-friend who turn up in the country as tourists. They may in fact be delightful company. On the other hand, they may well exploit your services as a host, guide, and interpreter, persuading you to impose on your Asian friends for train or theater tickets, hotel reservations, and other favors in a way that you would ordinarily never dream of doing, and then depart breezily to continue their way around the world, their only thanks a postcard from the French Riviera telling you how much you're missing by not being there.

1969

There's a Word for It

When the weather is really nice, I try to get out into the country for a walk. That's especially true in May, when the woods are at their finest and you know that the gloomy rainy season is looming just ahead. Since I make my living as a translator and work at home, I can usually arrange my schedule any way I like. So when we had a particularly fine day recently, I set off for Uji. There is a temple in the mountains southeast of Uji that I had been wanting to visit, called Kontai-ji, or the Temple of the Diamond and Womb Mandalas. The name derives from the colorful language of Esoteric Buddhism.

Getting off the Keihan Line at Uji, I began examining maps and bus schedules to see what bus I should take to get to the trail that leads to the temple. Some middle-aged, country-looking ladies sitting on a bench at the bus stop noticed my activities. "Where do you want to go, *ossan?*" they inquired cheerily. I was not entirely happy with that.

It is perfectly normal practice in Japanese to use kinship terms when addressing a stranger. In theory at least, therefore, there was nothing surprising in the fact that they had addressed me as *ossan,* or "uncle." But the trick in using kinship terms is to pick one that fits both the age of the speaker and the age of the person spoken to. In that sense, I did not think much of their choice of "uncle." Moreover, they had used not the standard Japanese word *ojisan* but its Kansai dialect equivalent, *ossan,* which, like the corresponding form for "aunt," *obahan,* tends to have facetious or derogatory connotations. In short, though it was certainly neighborly of the ladies to speak to me, I thought they could have chosen a form of address that sounded less like something out of a comedy routine.

Men in the Osaka area, when they want to speak to me but don't know my name, generally address me as *taishō*, which means something like "boss," or sometimes *magane no taishō*, "boss with glasses." The latter particularly delights me because it manages to be personalized without being impertinent. But *taishō* would probably not be an appropriate term for a well-mannered lady to use in addressing me. So as long as I live in the Kansai area and continue to get older rather than younger, I guess I had better get used to being called *ossan*. There have been times recently when I have been addressed by small children as "grandfather," so I know things could be worse.

"Where do you want to go?" they had asked. Whatever I thought about the manner of address, I ought to answer the question. But since I wasn't sure just where the trail started out from, I did not in fact know where I wanted to go. As a makeshift, I answered by naming the last stop on the bus line that went in the direction of the mountain where the temple is located. "I want to go to Iwamoto," I said.

The ladies nodded approvingly, no doubt pleased to discover that their uncle could speak intelligible Japanese and was not completely lost after all. Presently the Iwamoto bus pulled up and we all climbed aboard.

The bus wound up the gorge alongside the Uji River, passed the dam that has now turned the upper part of the gorge into a sinuous lake, and then swung off to follow a smaller river up into a narrow plain ringed by mountains. By the roadside I suddenly spotted a sign pointing out the trail to the mountain where I wanted to go. At the next stop I hurriedly gathered up my belongings and prepared to get off.

The ladies, who had been chatting quietly among themselves, sprang into action. "This isn't Iwamoto!" they warned me shrilly. "Iwamoto is two stops farther on!"

Such solicitude could not simply be ignored. On the other hand, I wasn't sure how to pronounce the name of the mountain where I was headed. Obviously, however, there was no time for lengthy explanation. I took the plunge. "I want to go to Shūhōzan," I said. The ladies stopped shrilling and settled back in their seats without comment as I hurried out of the bus.

I knew perfectly well how the name of the mountain is written. Indeed I had just seen it on the sign pointing out the trail. It is written with three Chinese characters that mean "Eagle Peak Mountain." I even knew where the name comes from—it comes from Gridhrakuta, "Eagle Peak" or "Vulture Peak" (English translations vary), the mountain in India where the Buddha preached the *Lotus Sutra*.

How could I know all that and still not know anything so elementary as the pronunciation, you may ask. Ah, but that is one of the special delights of the writing system in Japan. A single character or set of characters may have a variety of possible pronunciations, particularly in the case of place-names, and unless one has heard the name pronounced, one is never certain whether one will get it right or not. So, when pronouncing a place-name one is unsure of, one must always be prepared to meet with peals of laughter. I did not hear any such peals from the bus as it pulled away, so I guessed that this time I had been lucky. I remained happy in that conviction for fully an hour or more.

The trail to the mountain at first followed a paved road that threaded among pleasant clusters of farmhouses and past rows of intensely green tea plants that striped the hillsides. Then the paving ended, the trail passed through stone gateposts bearing the name of the temple up ahead, and started up a steep, narrow streambed through the trees.

I climbed for the next forty or fifty minutes. Sometimes the trail went almost straight up, at other times there were stretches that were nearly level. As I got up higher, I could hear birds singing in the trees on either side of the trail. One cry I identified as that of the *uguisu*, a sparrow-sized bird that, as anyone who has ever translated Japanese poetry knows, is called in English a bush warbler. Japanese say that the call of the bush warbler sounds like someone stammering out the word *Hokekyō*, one of the names for the *Lotus Sutra*. On a mountain named for that where the *Lotus Sutra* was preached, it seemed highly fitting that the birds should cry *Hokekyō*. But there was another cry that now and then came from the same direction as the bush warblers and was much shriller and more frenzied—a wild series of *toteeto-toteeto-toteeto* cries, as though the bird had suddenly lost its mind in an access of joy. What's that? I thought. The bush warbler making a different noise, or some other kind of bird? I practiced imitating the hysterical cry as I walked on, reminding myself to ask someone about it when I got home.

The Temple of the Diamond and Womb Mandalas turned out to be perched right on the very top of the mountain, elevation 685 meters. There seemed to be people stirring around in the living quarters of the temple, situated a little below the topmost level. But the halls and other religious buildings at the top, which included a handsome pagoda dating from the Kamakura period, were shut up tight. I stood for a while looking at the steep slopes that dropped off in all directions. Steel towers laden with power lines marched gigantically over a nearby ridge, lugging electricity from the Uji River Dam, but otherwise there was scarcely any sign of human activity. No one else was in the temple grounds, nor for that matter did I meet anyone on the trail going up or down.

At the entrance to the temple was a signboard with the history of the temple. It began by stating that the mountain, which I had called Shūhōzan, was called Jubusen. So I had in fact been phenomenally wrong, reading every one of the three characters in the name incorrectly. Presumably it was pity that had kept the ladies and the bus driver from laughing out loud at my performance. The sign also said that when Emperor Godaigo fled from Kyoto, he came to this mountain a while before establishing his headquarters at Mount Kasagi to the south of here.

I decided to go back down the mountain by a different trail, and for a while followed a dirt road that seemed to be used by the lumbermen who cut the stands of cedar planted on the mountain slopes. Then a sign pointed me off on a narrow path like the one I had come up by. Bush warblers once more sang in the branches, frilly iris-like flowers called *shaga* bloomed palely along the trail, and I could hear the sound of a stream bubbling at the bottom of a nearby ravine. I hurried down to it, the walk having made me very thirsty.

At home that evening, I got out Helen Craig McCullough's translation of the *Taiheiki*, the historical work that deals with the time of Emperor Godaigo, and looked to see if it said anything about his visiting the mountain where I had been. Emperor Godaigo, one will recall, was forced to flee Kyoto in 1331 when his plot to oppose the Kamakura shogunate came to light. According to the *Taiheiki*, after failing to gain support for his cause in Nara, he journeyed to Mount Jubu (Helen, unlike me, had known how to pronounce it correctly), but found it too remote from human habitation for his taste and left it for Mount Kasagi. That seemed sensible. At Mount Kasagi, he could at least look down from his craggy perch at the fields and hamlets along the Kizu River.

The same evening, I asked a Japanese friend if he knew the identity of the bird I had heard making such a wild cry, reproducing the cry for him as I had rehearsed it in the mountain. My friend showed immediate signs of comprehension. "*Uguisu no tani-watari,*" he said.

"So it *was* an *uguisu!*" I exclaimed.

He nodded.

"And what does *tani-watari* mean?"

"It's the cry the *uguisu* makes when he is crossing over from one valley to another."

I stared incredulously. A special word for one particular type of cry made by one particular species of bird? One has heard that some languages have highly specialized terminology in certain areas of reference, but this seemed too much to believe. I rushed to another room to consult my Japanese-English dictionary. There it was in Kenkyusha in unmistakable print: "*tani-watari*—the song of a bush warbler flying from valley to valley."

I poured myself a beer and settled back to go over in my mind the linguistic happenings of the day. *Ossan*—that had peeved me, and I thought how unexpectedly jarring language can be at times, even when the speaker means no harm. Shūhōzan—well, that could have happened to anybody. If I was going to let little mishaps like that worry me, I should never have left New York. But *uguisu no tani-watari*—there was a gem of language to cherish the rest of my life, and I thought excitedly of the moment when I might actually use it in a sentence. Its acquisition had made the day a stunning success.

1981

Sōjun

Sōjun was a monk who lived in a temple I used to visit south of Wakayama City in Japan. The first few times I went there, though, I never even saw him. He was always back in the kitchen or off working around the grounds.

I was on a sabbatical leave from Columbia University, living in Wakayama, and had decided, after a number of years of working in East Asian studies, that I ought to try Zen meditation. I had had connections with various Zen institutions when I lived in Kyoto in earlier days and had heard accounts of Zen training from people like Gary Snyder. At that time I could easily have taken up *zazen* if I had wanted to. But in those days I was in a big hurry to read old Chinese books and certain that I had no time to sit around meditating. It was a mistake, but not one that I'm sure I could have avoided at the time.

When I got to Wakayama in 1971 I began to think it was foolish not to try sitting once or twice just to see if I could do it. So when a professor of Wakayama University invited me to join a group of men and women who met in a local temple one afternoon a month to sit, I happily accepted. Later I drove down the peninsula with some of the group to visit the temple where Sōjun lived.

The temple has a *roshi* in residence and a regular *zendō*, or meditation hall. But it is not a registered training center for monks, and so there are rather few people living there—two or three older monks like Sōjun and various younger people who come and go. Also there are usually students or people who are studying for exams or recovering from an illness or otherwise want to be where it's quiet who drift in and out, so you never know who you will meet there. That's one of its attractions—unlike the big Zen temples in Kyoto, it's very informal and just about anyone who wants to can go and stay as long as he likes.

The first time I went we sat for a while in the meditation hall—my first experience sitting in a real *zendō*—and afterwards met the *roshi*. He was very friendly, not at all austere and inapproachable like the *roshi*s I'd met in Kyoto, and told us to come again any time. Why not? I thought, and started going down by myself on the train about once a week.

At first I just went in the daytime, sat by myself in the *zendō*, and then went home in the evening. But one day one of the monks said I should get the *roshi* to give me a koan. I hadn't been terribly serious about doing *zazen* in the first place, and I certainly never expected to embark on koan study. For one thing, I had only a few months left before I had to go back to America and I was sure I couldn't get far on a koan in that time. But again I thought, why not at least try? So the next time I went to the temple, I took some clothes along, determined to stay until I got a koan. That was when I first met Sōjun.

He was the *tenzō*, or cook, a very important person in a temple, since the way he does his job has a lot to do with whether the occupants remain in reasonably good humor. Sōjun was an excellent cook and meal planner, though he put out very simple fare. Most of the time the main dish was something like raw onions or cucumbers with vinegar or boiled spinach or eggplant, with an occasional sardine or bit of salted mackerel. His other specialty was chanting. He led the sutra chanting at the morning service, and in between sutras reeled off the long list of dead worthies to be commemorated in a wonderfully mellow and pliant voice.

Sōjun was a little man in his sixties with a large square

head and large knobby hands. He suffered from diabetes and got up at three every morning, an hour before the rest of the people in the temple get up, and gave himself an insulin shot. Then he spent the remainder of the hour pattering around in the dark and chanting before the various icons that are to be found scattered throughout the buildings and grounds of a large temple. During the day, he worked very hard around the grounds. He told me he had to work especially hard in order to work off the effects of the insulin, or something like that.

Though he never offered anything like formal advice, I learned a lot from Sōjun about Zen training. I remember one day when we were out pulling up weeds. There is a little stream that runs back of the bathhouse in a stone-lined channel and Sōjun told me to pull out all the weeds growing between the stones. I pulled away for awhile until I came to some very picturesque ferns sprouting from the channel wall. I said to Sōjun, "You don't want me to pull out these nice ferns, do you?"

"Pull out everything!" he said.

Lesson Number One: do not reason, do not think—do exactly as you are told. Of course, if I had stopped to consider, I would have realized that in a warm, damp place like Wakayama, the ferns are going to grow right back in anyway. But Zen people seem to have a real passion for weeding, for yanking up every last blade of grass and tiny bit of green in a walkway or courtyard. I wonder if that's not how that famous sand and rock garden at Ryōan-ji in Kyoto came into existence. It was probably laid out originally as a regular garden with plants and moss and later some particularly zealous monks got to working over it until all the green had disappeared.

Another time, we had just finished the noon meal and Sōjun told me to wipe off the long low table where we ate. As I did so, I noticed some bits of food under the table. I thought I would show how helpful I could be and I said, "Sōjun-san, while I'm at it, shall I sweep under the table?" "No," he replied with great firmness. "We almost never clean under there." Suddenly I remembered what I had learned years ago in the Navy. Do exactly what you are told to do—no less, no more.

I spent three years in the Navy as an enlisted man. Aside from the fact that there was a war going on, it was one of the happiest periods of my life. And I soon discovered that temple routine is a lot like being in the Navy, which I guess is one reason I don't find it as irksome as I might have expected, (though I've never tried living in a temple longer than a week at a time). For one thing, you never have to think what to do next. In the Navy there is always a bell or buzzer ordering you around, or a loudspeaker saying, "Now hear this!" In a Zen temple, a constant succession of bells, gongs, or wooden clappers, sounding in an assortment of patterns, direct your activities. At home I sit around wondering whether I ought to translate one more page or read one more chapter, and feeling guilty if I don't. But in the temple I'm never in doubt as to what I should be doing or when. It's very relaxing.

But to backtrack for a moment, I was so puzzled by Sōjun's remark about "we almost never clean under there" that I made discreet inquiries as to what it might mean. I was told that, since the temple is so large and at present so shorthanded, Sōjun felt that all efforts should be concentrated on keeping up outward appearances. In his view, the important thing was that visitors to the temple should be confronted with a neatly swept walk and a carefully weeded compound. A little dirt under a table that they would probably have no occasion to see anyway was a secondary matter. My informant added that I should perhaps regard this more as an expression of Wakayama folk wisdom than as a model for proper Zen procedure.

I recall one other memorable moment of instruction I received from Sōjun. We were having *sōsan*, when everyone in the temple is required to line up and go into the *roshi*'s room one by one for an interview. The procedure is a little different from that in the regular daily interview, which is voluntary. Instead of ringing the signal bell yourself, the person in charge rings it for you and you bow to him before going off to the *roshi*'s room. Then when you return, you stop in the corridor in front of the bell and kowtow.

But I had been back in America for a year and had forgotten the correct procedure. Sōjun was in charge, and when I was returning I started to pass him without kowtowing. He called to me, but I couldn't make out what it was he wanted me to do. Anyone else would probably have just said, "Dumb foreigner!" and let me do it wrong. Sōjun rose briskly, stepped out into the corridor, faced me in the proper direction and gently but firmly pushed me down until my head was touching the floorboards. Since then I have never forgotten the correct procedure.

Sōjun came from a Wakayama farm family, but he was trained at Shōkoku-ji in Kyoto, where he lived at Rinkō-in, a temple I happen to know quite well. He had a wife and family and for a time headed a temple of his own in the mountains in the southern part of Wakayama. But then there was some kind of mental illness and he left his family and tried to cure himself through various devotional practices associated with Esoteric Buddhism and mountain worship. I don't know when he returned to Zen life or when he moved to the temple where I met him.

He was very strong for his size. I recall the last work detail I did with him before I went back to America at the end of my sabbatical. Some big trees back of the temple had been cut down to make room for construction of a small hall dedicated to the long-nosed goblin type of deity known as a *tengu*. (Why a Zen temple would erect a *tengu* hall is too complicated a story to go into here.) It was August, the sun was blazing away, and I could barely manage to stagger down the steep slope with the pieces of pine log we were supposed to haul away. But Sōjun, though half my size and at least fifteen years older, hopped along under his piece of log like an animated gnome.

We often worked together around the grounds or drank tea together, but, though he was always smiling or cheerful, he seldom said anything. In particular, he didn't ask difficult questions about the differences between Christianity and Buddhism, as some of the other monks did, or get on my back about why wasn't I married or what did I do about sex.

He always went to the interview with the *roshi* each morning—I remember often sitting behind him in line and staring at the coarse, yellowed soles of his feet—but he never talked about koans or koan study. Only once I heard him remark on the subject. We used to gather after the morning interview to drink tea, and one morning one of the young monks was missing. Sōjun, who was making the tea, asked where he was and someone said, "He's sulking because he was so sure he was going to pass his koan and he didn't." Sōjun laughed and said, "Maybe he passed and went right out the other side." I'm not sure just what that remark means, if anything, but I frequently think of it when I am waiting in line to give my koan answer.

I had heard that Sōjun was very far along in koan study and might soon be receiving *inka*. But there was some trouble at the temple, things suddenly got very busy, and it was apparently too much for him. One cold morning in the middle of morning service he had a stroke.

I was living in Osaka by that time and didn't get to the temple very often, but I went down as soon as I heard the news. I was able to see him in the hospital the next day. He didn't speak but he put his knobby fingers around my hand and I think he recognized me. The next night around midnight they brought him back to the temple, dead. We laid him out in the main room and folded his gnarled hands over his chest. Death had shrunk him and his head and hands looked bigger than ever.

His daughter told me at the funeral that before he died he kept saying something about a "foreigner" waiting for him under a willow tree. I would suppose that the foreigner waiting for him must have been Shakyamuni, or perhaps Bodhidharma, though I like to think that some slight memory of me may have been reflected in the vision. Knowing him meant a lot to me.

1979

Rōhatsu Notes

Rōhatsu is a week of intensive meditation and training held in winter in Zen temples, usually in the first week of December. It is held then because Shakyamuni Buddha was supposed to have attained enlightenment at dawn of the eighth day of the twelfth month, though whether the twelfth month of the ancient Indian calendar corresponds to December is a doubtful point. I have attended *rōhatsu* for seven years at a temple in Wakayama belonging to the Rinzai branch of Zen. The temple holds what the *roshi*, or Zen master, who heads the temple calls a "family-style *rō-hatsu*," which means the schedule is less rigorous than that enforced in temples that have a *Sōdō*, or training center for monks. The most important difference is that we are allowed to get a regular night's sleep, whereas the more rigorous procedure followed in many temples all but prohibits sleep. Being in my fifties, I am sure I could not make it through a week of the strenuous kind. The following notes relate to my experiences over a number of years, though I have arranged them in the form of a single year's account.

Friday, November 30

I arrive at the temple about 5:30 in the afternoon and put my belongings in the big tatami room where most of us will sleep. The daily schedule for the *rōhatsu* period is posted and it looks like a good one.

A young monk named Ryūkō will be our *jikijitsu*, the man in charge of activities in the *zendō*, or meditation hall. He did it last year and was good. He does not keep us sitting for long stretches without a break, leads us in *kin-hin*, or walking exercise, from time to time, and does not hit too hard with the stick. Also he gives us a goodly amount of *samu*, or work, around the grounds. *Samu* is always a great relief during *rōhatsu* because it gives you a chance to exercise your legs and get rid of some of the aches and cricks that come from long sitting.

We have had various types of *jikijitsu* over the years I have been coming here—young ones who were eager but inexperienced, old ones who were just plain lazy. In particular I recall Chōgen, a little middle-aged monk from another temple who was staying here temporarily. He was a good *jikijitsu* except for two things: (1) a sitting period customarily lasts about thirty or forty minutes, after which the *jikijitsu* gives you a few minutes rest to stretch and move around in your seat before the next period begins. But Chōgen tended to go much longer without a break, and once kept us sitting an hour and a half before he broke the session. If your legs are troubling you, that can be pure hell; (2) the *keisaku*, or stick, is ordinarily administered only to people who request it, though the *jikijitsu* may beat people who are drowsing or otherwise at fault, or as a form of friendly encouragement. But Chōgen beat in anger, something I had never seen before or since. On the morning of the fourth day he began yelling hysterically at a student who had been in bed for two days with a stomach upset, accusing him of malingering, and gave him eight or ten hard blows on each shoulder. Then he screamed at a young monk for his careless attitude and beat him the same way. Finally he beat another student, for no apparent reason at all. It was an ugly performance and one that gave me second thoughts about traditional Zen training methods, though perhaps I overreacted.

The moon is nearly full and when I go to the meditation hall around 7 it is racing in and out of big billowy gray clouds. The temple is still, dark, and cold, as usual on the night before *rōhatsu* when people have not yet arrived. And, as usual, I begin to have dark feelings of anxiety and foreboding and ask myself why I get myself into situations like this. But later Ryūkō arrives, along with several other laymen like myself who will be here for the week, and I feel less apprehensive.

I took a bath after leaving the meditation hall at 9. At first I used to bathe every day, since it is allowed at this temple during *rōhatsu*. But last year it dawned on me that, though the bath helps to ease the pain in legs and shoulders, when one returns to the meditation hall after a bath, the pain is worse than ever. Why? Obviously because the hot bath stimulates circulation and all the offended nerves begin to scream. So it should be likewise obvious that the thing to do is not to bathe or otherwise stimulate the nerves, but let them get as nearly numb as possible from the cold. I followed this procedure last year, not taking a bath all week, and found it a great improvement. So this will probably be the last bath I take until the final night. These little tricks help so much to ease one through—it's too bad one has to discover them all for oneself, and that it takes me, at least, so long to do so.

Saturday, December 1

Up at 4 with the big bell, then *chōka*, the morning service of sutra chanting. Then, because this is the first of the month, we race around in the dark to several other parts of the temple and compound for special chanting services. This over, we go to the meditation hall. Other years we have had a *dokusan*, or private interview, with the *roshi* at 5, but he is getting old and is not very strong, so this has been eliminated this year. We will have *dokusan* at 7:30, 10, and 4, with *sōsan* at 8. *Sōsan* is almost the same as *dokusan* except that, whereas *dokusan* is optional, everyone must go to *sōsan*.

Weather damp and chilly. In work period we clean up litter where pine trees have been cut down. Practically all the pines on the temple grounds have been killed by the *matsukui-mushi*, an insect that is wiping out the pines all over Japan. One after another the beautiful old trees, some of them hundreds of years old, have to be cut down, leaving the grounds stark and devastated. But there seems to be nothing that can be done. One can only hope the other trees will grow up quickly to fill the emptiness.

Pain in my back at late afternoon sitting session, probably due to the fact that I am not yet accustomed to the yard work and the routine in general. I'm reminded of how quickly the mind becomes foggy with prolonged sitting, particularly when one is fatigued. One is constantly forgetting even a short, simple koan, and in its place come all sorts of ridiculous and unrelated words and phrases to lead the mind astray and block concentration.

Bad evening, more pain in back. The regular evening *teishō*, or lecture, by the *roshi* is on the *Zenkai ichiran*, a collection of Confucian axioms and pronouncements arranged like Zen koans. In addition, as in other years, the *roshi* is reading from Tōrei's instructions for *rōhatsu*, an Edo period text in classical Japanese that makes next to no sense to me when read aloud. *Roshi* is having trouble with his eyes and takes a long time at the reading. He always tells us jokingly that *teishō* is a good time to take a little nap, and with material like this, I would have to agree with him.

A few local people come for the evening sitting session, *teishō*, and *sōsan*. This year there is a nurse, a young man from the shipyard, and some school teachers. Also a number of people have come from Osaka for the weekend. After the evening schedule is over, we gather to drink *amazake*, a very mild, sweet home-brewed sake, and tea.

Sunday, December 2

Cold and very windy, wind howling through the meditation hall. Koan still going very badly—I am apparently not coming anywhere near the right answer and can't tell why or how to change my approach. I was afraid my legs would be a problem in the last hour before lunch, but then suddenly I reached one of those wonderful plateaus of calm. It's not that the pain ceases, but that you recede from it, you move up a little higher where you can look down on it and say with confidence, this much I can handle. I hope I can get there again this afternoon. Ryūkō has been going around the hall and giving everyone a beating with the stick, but impartially and without emotion, as it should be. Some people make a very impressive smack, but I just sound like an old sofa cushion. Is this because I have on so many layers of clothing, or just because the blows sound different when they are at a distance from you?

Yesterday at *samu* someone pointed out some *shii*, or pasania nuts, that had fallen on the main approach to the temple and showed me how to eat one. Today I went and picked up some more and ate them. They are very small, brownish-black, and the kernel tastes something like a filbert. Eating them makes me think of Bashō and Ryōkan and other Japanese writers who talk about pasania trees and nuts, and it pleases me very much to think that now I too have eaten of the fruit of the pasania.

Monday, December 3

A clear, still morning. Many people had come from Osaka to attend the sessions on Saturday night and Sunday, but they have all gone back to Osaka. We are down to just six, including Anne Marie, a French woman who teaches in Kyoto, and old Mr. Yamagiwa, a retired company president in his seventies who sits in the meditation hall with a little lap robe over his knees. (He is the oldest member of the group; the youngest is the twelve-year-old son of one of the businessmen from Osaka.) I am wearing a heavy kimono and *hakama* skirt that wraps around my legs, so I manage to keep warm most of the time, though on very cold mornings I sometimes get the shakes.

———

The food always tastes so good at *rōhatsu!* It's amazing that you can work up such an appetite just doing *zazen.* Of course the work sessions around the grounds and the regular schedule help the hunger. For *shukuza,* or breakfast, we have been having rice gruel with sweet potatoes in it, which is delicious. Today for *saiza,* or lunch, we had some particularly good *udon,* or wheat noodles, that someone brought from Shikoku. They are served in big pots of boiling water and eaten dipped in a sesame-flavored sauce. Aside from eating, the other great pleasure at *rōhatsu* is the wonderful feeling when you crawl into bed at the end of the day and stretch out your weary legs, knowing that in a moment you will be sound asleep. But of course one really shouldn't be going to bed at all during *rōhatsu.*

Good afternoon. I washed my clothes so I will have a clean change of underwear and shirt to put on the last day. Had bad pain in my back in late afternoon sitting session, but then recovered. Just a little shift in the arrangement of your cushions or posture can clear up the pain. *Remember* this. The pain does not necessarily get progressively worse with time—it sometimes goes the other way. *You will not be tried beyond endurance.*

Tuesday, December 4

A rainy morning. Our work session consists of indoor jobs mopping corridors, cleaning toilets, mending paper panels that have become torn. As I sit in the meditation hall afterward, I can smell the *karin,* or Chinese quince, that grows just outside the window. This time of the year it has big waxy yellow fruit on it that gives off a lovely spicy odor, as though the tree were trying to cheer us along in our endeavors. There are several new people in the group, including a Mexican who is studying Japanese at Tenri University in Nara. He doesn't seem to have had much experience sitting and looks as though he's having a hard time. I am reminded of the time some years ago when a young American who was teaching English in Wakayama showed up for *rōhatsu.* I don't think he knew just what he was getting into, and I suspect he had quite a lot of pain, but he gamely stuck it out to the end. One day at work session he confided to me that he wasn't making much progress with his koan. "I told the *roshi* that I didn't find it a very meaningful question!" he announced. I gulped. "And what did the *roshi* say?" I asked. "He said 'Talk to Watson about it.'" I told him that if he found the question so meaningless, why didn't he try giving a meaningless answer. I don't know how it came out.

———

If there is one thing the participants in a *rōhatsu* loathe and detest, it is visitors to the temple who disrupt the schedule. Of course in a very strict temple, *all* visitors are turned away during *rōhatsu,* but for various reasons it is impossible to do that here. So people at times come in and take up the *roshi*'s time and throw the schedule off. To a bunch of cold, hungry people sitting in the meditation hall with aching legs, even a ten- or fifteen-minute delay in the bell that signals *dokusan* or the gong or clappers that call us to meals can be agonizing. Meanwhile the tinkle of the visitor's carefree laughter carries across the compound to our ears, while we sit with our lapful of pain and curse the intruder.

As usual at *rōhatsu*, much of the *roshi*'s conversation when we see him at *teishō* or tea-drinking time consists of accounts of how tough the *rōhatsu* routine is at this or that temple, where they beat people the most, where the snow comes right in the meditation hall, etc. This is the kind of talk Zen people seem to relish, like old soldiers or sailors exchanging stories about which assignments or bases are toughest. The other type of talk most often heard from the *roshi* is of former *roshi*s who were famous for the rigorous training they underwent, their youthful zeal, or their contempt in later years for power, authority, position. This seems to sum up the Zen ideal as it has been handed down, something that you feel has a living connection with the past. But it is the kind of ideal that will never have much popular appeal. Zen people have always known that, of course. They repeatedly say that one can never expect to find any more than a handful of real Zen men or women around at any given time. I suppose that's why they make so little effort to proselytize. There's a feeling that the people who are really suited for Zen will somehow find their own way to the religion, and that there is little point in talking to the others.

Wednesday, December 5

Funny how the different days of the seven-day period have their distinctive "feel," depending upon their place in the order. After the hush and loneliness of the 30th, one is happy to be launched into the first day. The second day can be very tiring as one is adjusting to the new hours of sleeping and rising and the daily routine. At this point it is all *noborizaka*, or "uphill climb," as the *roshi* constantly reminds us, and he himself is accordingly tough in the way he treats us. One sees the days passing but hardly ventures to look ahead at how many are left. Then on the 4th you go "over the hump," and there is a mood of restrained elation. By this time it is apparent that you are going to be able to make it to the end. With this realization comes a kind of letdown—is this all there is? At the same time, discipline seems to grow a little laxer and the *roshi* becomes a bit more benign. Now we are into the 5th, which means that the end is approaching. More and more one finds oneself thinking about things one wants to eat or drink or do when one gets on the "outside" again. It's not so much that one misses such particular items of food or drink. What one misses is the opportunity to exercise the will, to decide for oneself what one will eat or do. Now that I've given up smoking, about the only opportunity I have to make a choice during *rōhatsu* is when I decide whether or not to have a drink of water, and that's not a terribly exciting decision.

It finally happened—what I'm always fearful of: we got caught in a session that ran overtime and reduced us—or me, at least—to the state of a painful cripple. It happened, as these things usually do, because the schedule got a little off. Ten o'clock *dokusan* didn't begin until around 10:15, which meant we got back to the meditation hall about 10:40 instead of 10:30. The remaining time until lunch at 11:30 should have fallen into two sessions with a break in the middle. But because it was late, Ryūkō decided to run it all together into one 50-minute session. At another point in the day that might not have bothered me, but coming at the end of the morning, it did me in. I have said that one is not tried beyond endurance, and I will stick by that. But one is at times pushed a lot nearer the borderline than one would like to be. Toward the end, a kind of numbness set in, but I'm very disappointed in myself that I can't seem to get better control of the pain as I have in previous years. It rained throughout the morning, and it is usually delightful to sit in the meditation hall and hear the soft rustle of the rain. But when you are in pain and listening intently in hopes you will hear the *jikijitsu* picking up his bell and clappers to signal a break, the sound of the rain can be cruelly deceiving. The drops plocking from the eaves seem to be speaking to you, and what they say is nothing nice.

And out of all this ache and fret comes a splendid discovery. When I had calmed down from my outrage, I began to wonder why I should have so much more pain than at times in the past. When I went to the meditation hall for the 1 to 2 sitting, I tried putting my right leg not high up on my left calf, as I ordinarily do at home or when sitting for short periods, but farther over into my crotch so the right ankle bone is not resting on my left leg. Result: the pain is cut at least in half, if not more. Why didn't I think of this earlier? Why can't someone teach me these things? Again the point to remember is that a very slight change in posture or sitting arrangement can make things enormously easier at times. Be prepared to bear up when there is nothing else you can do, especially when caught in a bad posture in the midst of a session when movement is out of the question. But at the same time never stop experimenting to see if there isn't a better, more comfortable way to sit. Now I feel I can face the rest of the day!

This afternoon we worked up back of the main garden, cleaning up more pine mess. The maples around the upper pond have turned a very beautiful color this year, almost making you forget the ravaged pines. In addition, the *tsu-wabuki* are in bloom, low-standing plants with dark shiny green leaves and stalks of yellow aster-like flowers that seem to glow in the shadows.

While we were working, a very friendly white dog appeared and frolicked around where we were. When we finished and went to the meditation hall, he came right along and wanted to climb up on the platform. Our stern shouts and commands to get out were taken as a joke and he only bounced around all the more, until we finally had to drive him out and shut the doors of the hall. Then Anne Marie, who had been working somewhere else around the grounds, came along and, not knowing what was going on, opened the doors and in no time our friend was bouncing around the hall again.

Thursday, December 6

The temple is very lively today, as this is the day the local farmer-parishioners bring rice and daikon radishes as their contribution to the temple. This temple serves various functions and various different groups in the community, so activities like this have to go on even though it is *rōhatsu*. (One year we had an elaborate funeral right in the middle of *rōhatsu* when an elderly parishioner died suddenly.) The contributions are brought to the big entrance hall, where the donors' names are written down in a book. The daikon are neatly tied in bundles of three or four radishes each. This afternoon at work session we will rig bamboo poles under the eaves of the shed behind the kitchen and hang the daikon on the poles, where they will dry for a few days before being put into barrels for pickling. The rice donations will be carted off by a man from the local rice store who has come with his truck. He will store the rice for the temple and bring it when it is needed.

───────

At *yakuseki*, the evening meal, we had some of the daikon that was brought today, boiled in broth with fried bean curd. It tasted indescribably good, particularly as it is a cold evening. If you tried to fix it at home it would never taste this good. I think one reason the food at the temple tastes so good is that everything is cooked in big batches, enough to serve twenty or thirty people. You never know when people may turn up unexpectedly at mealtime, so there has to be plenty of food on hand. And if there are leftovers, they are all dumped in together and taste even better the second day.

Since the *rōhatsu* is almost over, and since tonight, unlike so many other nights, I do not have to spend time looking up a *go*, or capping phrase, to take to *dokusan* in the morning, I decided to do a little *yaza*, or "night sitting." It is optional, but if one is really earnest in his *rōhatsu* practice he ought to be doing it every night for several hours or more instead of going to bed, either on the veranda or in the garden or meditation hall. But I'm the kind of person who works at things slowly and steadily rather than in great bursts of activity—in my college days I never stayed up all night studying for an exam or finishing a term paper—and anyway I'm afraid if I do *yaza* I may be too tired to get through the following day properly. But tonight I was feeling a little guilty, as I know that others of our group do *yaza* each night in the meditation hall, so I went off to join them for a while.

It was bright moonlight outside, but the hall was very dark, with only the two small altar lamps burning at the rear of the hall. I could make out the dark shapes of several sitters but it was impossible to tell who they were. The night was extraordinarily still—no trains going by, no cars, no planes, and more unusual, no owl hoots or other bird or animal noises. I sat for about thirty minutes. I would like to say that the experience was moving or mysterious, but I'm afraid spooky is about the best I could say of it. When I left around 10, the others were still in their places, leaving me feeling as guilty as I had been to begin with. One good effect of the *yaza* was that I got quite chilled, so that the bed felt even better than ever when I crawled in.

Friday, December 7

The final day, when we will have the "last" of everything— last morning service, last morning work period, etc. The chanting at the morning service, incidentally, has been going a little better for me these last few days. The monk who sets the pace usually goes so fast I can barely keep up, particularly on the Kannon chapter of the *Lotus Sutra*, the longest piece, which comes right at the beginning when I'm still only half-awake. But someone must have spoken to him, as he has slowed down the tempo a little.

By this time one is so accustomed to the routine that one no longer has any great desire to see the *rōhatsu* end. But of course it does, and the last day is usually marked by various interruptions and changes in the schedule and the departure of people who have a long trip home and must be at work tomorrow. After many tries, I have at last gotten the right capping phrase to wind up the koan I have been working on and am now started on a new koan.

Afternoon work session back of the kitchen, the last day of *rōhatsu* rapidly fading away. We were weeding and cleaning around the back steps, a flight of rough stone steps going down the slope from the kitchen garden, a sunny spot, just right for a cold day like this. The sky was superbly clear and blue and the view out over the valley was very lovely. The rice has long since been harvested and the fields are planted now with winter crops of lettuce, beans, and garlic.

I wonder why all through the week I have thought repeatedly of New York, New Jersey, scenes in the Hudson Valley, riding on the Jersey Central and watching the little towns go by—in the days when the windows of the Jersey Central were clean enough to see out of. I don't especially wish to be in those places right now, but somehow it is indescribably pleasant when sitting in the meditation hall to have memories of them come floating up in my mind. Particularly memories of New York as it was when I was a student, drinking beer in the San Remo, shopping for green vegetables and Italian sausage on Madison Street near my apartment, the way the Third Avenue El came clattering down from Chatham Square, stooping to get under the Brooklyn Bridge. Perhaps sitting helps to release these happy recollections from the past.

All the sitting and *teishō* and *sōsan* have come to an end and it is time for the *Jōdōe*, or Attainment of Enlightenment Ceremony that commemorates Shakyamuni's enlightenment and brings the *rōhatsu* to a close. A little after 9 in the evening we file into the Hattō, or Dharma Hall, the main hall of the temple, and line up in two rows facing each other at right angles to the altar and the tall dais at the back of the hall upon which sits the statue of Shakyamuni Buddha in the center with attendant statues on either side.

The *hōku*, or Dharma drum, begins to sound. It is a large round drum that rests on a stand in the northeast corner of the hall. The beater stands in front of it and beats it with two drumsticks. The beating is quite elaborate, alternating between thumps on the head of the drum in a syncopated pattern of te-tum-tum-tum-tum that increases in speed, and a wild rattling noise made by passing the drumsticks rapidly over the round metal knobs that decorate the rim of the drum. The alternating clatter of this and the resounding bongs from the head of the drum create an atmosphere of tension and excitement. The drumming continues until the *roshi* and his attendant enter the hall.

The *roshi* stands facing the altar in front of a large square of cloth that is spread on the tile floor. After a bow, he walks around the cloth and up to the incense burner on the altar. The attendant stands beside him, his head bowed low, and with a great flourish of his arm removes the lid of the lacquer box of incense he is carrying and holds up the box. The *roshi* takes incense and drops it in the censer.

The *roshi* and attendant move back to their former position in front of the cloth. Two men in robes of *komusō* monks begin to play on vertical flutes of the kind called *shakuhachi*s. Everyone chants the *Daihi Emmon Bukai Jinshu*, a Sanskrit text that pledges devotion to the Three Treasures—the Buddha, the doctrine, and the religious community. The *roshi* removes his *zagu*, a piece of cloth that is folded over his shoulder, spreads it out on top of the larger cloth, steps out of his big red-and-white pointed Chinese shoes, and performs three prostrations on the cloth. At his age it is hard for him to get up and down. We watch apprehensively, wishing there were some way we could help.

He goes to the altar again and burns more incense. He returns to his former position and in a loud, drawn-out voice intones a Chinese poem in seven-character *chüeh-chü*, or quatrain form, that he has composed for the occasion. He says he does not like the job of composing such poems in Chinese because the prosodic rules are so exacting. From what I can get of the words, the poem seems to say something about the light of the Buddha's great achievement shining down over the centuries to us.

The *shakuhachi*s begin to play again as the *roshi* and his attendant withdraw. Then we file forward one by one to bow before the statue of Shakyamuni.

Because the images in a Zen Dharma hall are placed so high up above the floor, they tend to look more remote and aloof than the images in many other types of Buddhist halls. They are not hidden away behind doors and curtains, as are many of the images in temples of Esoteric Buddhism, but neither do they loom down on you in an awesome manner as do the giant images in the old Nara temples. They just seem rather far away, not to be taken particular notice of, which is perhaps appropriate in view of the nature of Zen teaching.

But on this one night, perhaps because of the repeated offerings of incense made to him, the music, the poem, all in his honor, Shakyamuni seems to come to life, to glow in his gilt and take on an air of solemn importance. It is *his* accomplishment we are celebrating, *his* example we have, in our meager way, been attempting to emulate all week, and as I look up at him sitting there, I am suddenly moved. I guess it is the only point in the whole *rōhatsu* procedure when I have a specifically religious, or at least pious and reverent, feeling and it only lasts a moment. Yet I look forward to it each year, and come away with a sense of having been in touch momentarily with something of immense value and significance.

———

I am back in the room where we sleep and the clappers are sounding to call us to the party that comes at the very end. We will have *oden*, a stew made of bean curd and assorted vegetables simmered in broth, and beer and sake to drink. Tomorrow I will take an early train back to Osaka.

1981

My Mansion on the Hill

The piano teacher and I both started off in grand style. In February of 1957, when my Japanese roommate and I moved from our previous lodging to the mansion on the hill, it was agreed that we would have the use of the three Japanese-style rooms on the ground floor—what had originally been the main living room of the house, plus two smaller rooms off it—while the piano teacher would have the small Japanese-style room next to the kitchen, which we were to share, and the ballroom. At least I guess it was a ballroom: a vast, high-ceilinged Western-style room with a stonework fireplace, dark wood-paneling, a tapestry, and a tiny balcony that jutted out at second-story level in one corner of the room and was evidently intended to accommodate a trio of midget musicians. The long dark corridor that ran from the front entrance past my rooms to the ballroom was in the same vaguely Tudor style, with a window of amber-colored leaded glass and carved wooden arms that stuck out of the wall and held light fixtures with flame-shaped bulbs.

Though I had not met the piano teacher before, she and I both happened to move on the same day. My modest arrival, involving only a small load of books and belongings that an iceman friend kindly carted over for me in his truck, was completely overshadowed, however, by the spectacle of the grand piano. While the piano teacher fretted and the neighborhood children milled around in excitement, a crew of workmen struggled all afternoon with rollers and tackle to haul it up the long flight of stone steps that led to the house, maneuver it through the front door, and install it in the ballroom.

Mrs. Uchida, the landlady, rushed here and there supervising the cleaning women who had been hired for the day to scrub the rooms we were to occupy, and even lit the huge gas water-heater that supplied hot water to all the taps in the house, though she assured me that it was far too expensive to use except on special occasions. "Before the war, when my husband was alive and we had plenty of money," she told me, "we used to have the third largest gas bill in all of Kyoto!"

Mr. Uchida, a prosperous Japanese businessman, had built the mansion in the early 1930s, after returning from several years as his company's representative in England, and had gone to considerable expense to incorporate into it the foreign tastes he had acquired abroad. His widow now lived with her married daughter in a smaller house next door and rented out the large house to an assortment of Japanese and foreign tenants.

When I moved in, the third floor, one very large room over the ballroom that had been fitted with a makeshift kitchen, was occupied by an American named Hall, his Japanese wife, and their little son Stephan. Miss Winton and Miss Hopper, two middle-aged English missionaries, lived in the Japanese-style rooms on the second floor, directly above me, while the piano teacher and I together accounted for most of the ground floor. There were two baths at the rear of the ground floor, one with a large tile tub, which Mrs. Uchida said was too costly to heat up, and another with a smaller wooden tub. Any tenant who cared to pay his share of the gas required to heat it was free to use the latter, but after trying it a few times, my roommate and I decided that the public bath nearby, with its spacious pools and unlimited quantities of hot water, was a much better buy.

In addition to these tenants, there was a student who lived in what had been a maid's room off the main entrance. He seemed to sleep most of the day and at night went out to play mahjong with friends. Behind the house, in a pair of very small rooms designed for use in the tea ceremony and connected to the house by a narrow passageway, lived a young Kyoto University instructor who was working on a doctorate in Thomist philosophy. I did not even know he was there until one day when I happened to wander through the grove of bamboo back of the house and suddenly came on him, sitting in his cell and poring over the works of the Church Fathers. He had closed off the passageway and came and went through a back gate. I seldom saw him except when I had occasion to call him to the phone.

The only telephone in the house was located in the main hall just outside the room I used for a study. Tenants who made outgoing calls were bound by honor to deposit ten yen a call in the cardboard box beside it, but shortly after I moved in Mrs. Uchida, expressing profound dissatisfaction at the sums she found in the box, had the instrument replaced by an automatic pay phone. I soon discovered that, by an unwritten law of proximity, the person who occupied my part of the house was expected to answer incoming calls. As a result I quickly became familiar with the other tenants, dashing down the hall several times a day to shout their names up the stairwell or, in the case of the Kyoto University instructor, to bang on the heavy wooden door that closed off the passageway to the tea room in hopes he would hear me.

Miss Winton and Miss Hopper received the largest number of calls. Both had been nurses and licensed midwives in England before becoming missionaries, and some of their phone calls were concerned with medical services that they performed for the local missionary community.

(The law of proximity not only required me to answer the phone but also, unless I left my study, to listen in on the ensuing conversations.) Most of their calls, however, came from a young Japanese woman named Miss Endo, the first convert they had made since their arrival in Kyoto the year before. Miss Endo had just gone to work as the cook for a German family in Kyoto and, in an effort to impress her new employers, was apparently overtaxing her ability. Almost every afternoon about five-thirty she would call up to ask in a tremulous voice if I would please get Miss Winton or Miss Hopper to the phone. Having shouted the message up to the second floor and returned to my room, I would hear one of them on the phone explaining in earnest Japanese how to keep the cake from falling or what to do to the roast next. The instructions always ended with an injunction to Miss Endo to remain calm and trust in the Lord. But Miss Endo's faith was as yet embryonic, and it often required two or three more calls before the German family's dinner finally got on the table.

Miss Winton and Miss Hopper were clearly well qualified to advise Miss Endo on culinary matters. They told me that their main reason for being in Kyoto was so they could study at the language school for foreigners there. But when they were not occupied with tutors, homework, or practical workouts with Miss Endo on the phone, they devoted themselves to what seemed to be their real love, cooking. They often brought me samples—excellent pies, tarts, and jams, which I accepted as my fee for the telephone answering service. Later, when the weather got hot and we shared the big icebox, I had daily glimpses of the various dishes they prepared.

The icebox, a relic from a former tenant, rested in the dark recesses of the unused bath so that the water from the melted ice could run out the drain. Its use was urged on us by Mrs. Uchida, though it was far too big for our needs and required an alarming quantity of ice. Only after we had unwarily accepted her generosity and used it for several months did she explain about the monthly rental fee. This sort of spurious kindness caught me off guard on another occasion as well, when at her suggestion I planted some vegetables in a plot of ground at the back of the house and subsequently found myself dunned for a "vegetable patch fee." She pictured herself as a helpless widow whom all the world was conspiring to do in, and had evidently concluded that her only defense was to do it in first. "Tea ceremony, flower arrangement, the accomplishments of an old-style Japanese lady—these I learned from childhood," she confided to me. "But when it comes to money matters, I'm utterly lost!"

Mr. Hall rated next in number of calls. He was a quiet, soft-spoken young man who had been stationed in Japan with the U.S. Army and had returned after his discharge to marry the Japanese girl he had been going with and "have another look at the country." He spent his days taking photographs—beautiful color shots of Kyoto which he called me up to his room from time to time to see—though what he planned to do with them I never learned. Most of his phone calls came from the local photography store that did his developing. His Japanese was scrappy, but spoken with such an authentic accent that, overhearing him on the phone in the hall, I often mistook him for a Japanese. He was an amateur musician, which perhaps had something to do with his acute ear for language, and played the flute, as I discovered one warm spring evening when I opened my window and heard the languid strains of "The White Peacock" floating down from the third floor.

Mrs. Hall was from Tokyo, dyed her hair a reddish tint, and did little to disguise her disdain for the local housewives who gathered daily in front of their houses at the foot of the steps to sweep, stretch pieces of kimono mate-

rial in the sun to dry, and stand around gossiping. They re-
taliated by staring at her mercilessly when she passed and
clearly concluding the worst.

The Halls' two-year-old son Stephan, brought up in a bi-
lingual atmosphere of Japanese and English, took little interest in either but spoke most of the time in a melodious
tongue of his own invention. His real interest was insects,
and in their case he had made an exception by acquiring
from his mother an extensive Japanese vocabulary of insect names. From my study I would often hear him wandering alone up and down the dark corridor, calling softly
to his favorites—"Spider! Moth! Fly!"

The piano teacher, an attractive but rather nearsighted
woman of about thirty, surprisingly got the fewest calls of
all—only a rare long-distance call from someone she referred to as "a gentleman friend in Kobe." She had insisted
when she moved in that she must have the ballroom to
give piano lessons in, and so her ten-year-old daughter, Yoshiko, could have a place to practice ballet. Mrs. Uchida
was delighted to comply, since none of the other tenants
had shown any interest in paying for the use of so dreary
and improbable a room. Perhaps the pupils the piano
teacher had counted on simply failed to materialize; at
any rate, no one ever to my knowledge came to the house
for lessons. Someone in the ballroom played "A Maiden's
Prayer" on the grand piano two or three times a day, and
Yoshiko occasionally pirouetted through its arched doorway and down the hall in the way that ballet-minded little
girls often do. But unless the piano teacher was a great deal
better off than she appeared to be, none of us could see how
these activities alone could justify the price we knew Mrs.
Uchida was charging her for the room.

In addition to the piano teacher and her daughter, there
was an old woman who cooked meals for them. She had
been introduced as Yoshiko's grandmother, but Yoshiko

talked back to her so ferociously that, even allowing for the unusual degree of sassiness that Japanese tolerate in young children, we concluded that the old woman could hardly be her real grandmother. More likely she was some distant and indigent relative whom Yoshiko had learned from her mother to treat with contempt.

My own phone calls were likewise few, and considering what little use I made of the phone, I soon got fed up with my duties as official answerer for the house. Nor was this my only objection to the first-floor rooms.

The house, in the northeastern suburbs of Kyoto, was perched on the side of a hill facing south. The slope was planted with pines and cherries, and during April my roommate and I had a more spectacular view of shimmering branches and petals scattering in the breeze than most of the people who battled crowds at the city's famed cherry-viewing spots. But in May and June, with the onset of the rainy season, the drawbacks of a hillside site in Japan became apparent. Water oozed out of every corner of the grounds and the house became permeated with dampness, particularly the shady ground-floor rooms that we occupied. When we folded up the sleeping mats in the morning, we could see their outline on the tatami, dark rectangles in a meadow of gray mold that had sprung up all around us in the night.

With the dampness, which did strange things to the muscles in my back, came new varieties of insects, among them the long, ugly centipedes that can inflict such a painful sting. Fortunately, it is beyond the power of a centipede to tread softly, and I could usually detect their presence by the scrape of their feet on the straw mats or paper panels, though that hardly made me any less apprehensive. Also, I concluded that the rooms were too large for our needs, and too expensive, though Mrs. Uchida assured me she was charging barely half of what she had gotten from the

American Army couple who occupied them previously. When it developed that Thomistic studies were going to provide the Kyoto University instructor with an opportunity to spend a year at Harvard, we asked her if we could move into his rooms at the back of the house. After some dickering over price, she consented.

An interesting succession of tenants followed in our place. First came a sallow young man described by Mrs. Uchida as the president of an artificial flower company. He was said to be recovering from an illness and spent all his time lying in bed and watching television. An older woman cooked his meals and looked after him. He invited me in one day to chat and asked what I knew about Christmas decorations, which his company was planning to manufacture. After telling him all I could recall from my childhood on that subject, I inquired about his illness. He said his stomach felt oppressively heavy and his legs wobbled when he tried to walk, though he admitted that none of the doctors had been able to find anything definitely wrong. I pointed out that both symptoms might come from spending so much time in bed, but he only patted his abdomen gravely and said, "Something not right down here!" Mrs. Hall astutely guessed that he was merely hiding out from creditors, and she was apparently right, because after a month or so he got out of bed, packed his things and left.

He was followed by an American studying Shingon Buddhism who shook my hand vigorously and said he was sure he was going to like the rooms, though he hadn't settled the exact price with Mrs. Uchida—in fact, if he had understood her Japanese correctly, she had hinted he might not have to pay any rent at all if he would teach her grandson a little English conversation. This sounded so unlike the Mrs. Uchida we knew that we all waited in anticipation for the altercation we were sure would ensue when the

113

first of the month came around. It took place in the garden, where we could get a good view of the contestants from our windows, and ended with the American ungallantly thumbing his nose at the old woman and moving out the same day. She, in her imperfect and somewhat confused understanding of Western customs, took the gesture to be unspeakably more vile than it is usually thought to be, and was in a rage for a week. "I've met a lot of people from your country," she informed me acidly, "but none as low class as that!"

The group that moved into the downstairs rooms next were among the liveliest we had ever had. I say group because they were not a family but a firm, engaged, according to the large sign they posted at the gate, in the making of burglar alarms. They had moved up from Osaka and consisted of the president of the firm, his two small children, a pretty young housekeeper, and three young men who did the actual work of making the alarms—all seven of them, plus their equipment, installed in the three rooms my roommate and I had occupied. Mrs. Uchida protested vehemently about the sign, but they explained that it was required by law since the downstairs of her house was now technically a factory. They strung one of their alarms around the outside of the house and showed us all how to get in and out of the gate without tripping it. We could now rest easy in our beds, they said—and so we thought until one muggy September night about a month later.

I was wakened around 2 A.M. by the sound of children wailing. At first I supposed the centipedes had at last claimed a victim, and was about to go back to sleep. But when I heard the other people in the house racing around and talking excitedly, I got up and went down to the door of the burglar-alarm factory, where I found a group gathered. The young housekeeper was explaining that there had been a Peeping Tom in the garden. Only not exactly a

Peeping Tom, because he had marched right into her room. "He said what he wanted, just like that!" she exclaimed breathlessly. A quick-witted girl, she explained that his request was impossible because of the two children sleeping in the same room. When he persisted, she said that, since it was time to wake the children and take them to the bathroom anyway, she would move their bedding into the next room and put them to bed there. Her visitor simple-mindedly agreed to this procedure, and when she had gotten the children up and out into the hall, she pinched them as hard as she could until their screams woke the household.

The company president was out of town on business and the piano teacher was inexplicably absent, but the rest of us were now all assembled, fidgeting in our nightclothes and debating what should be done. The children, having ceased their wailing, were falling asleep on their feet, and the visitor had of course fled long ago. We concluded there was nothing to do until daylight revealed whether he had left any tracks in the garden. While Miss Winton and Miss Hopper assured me they would have required no such devious stratagem to deal with a visitor of *that* type, we dispersed to our rooms, leaving the old woman from the piano teacher's standing by her door, shaken and pale, muttering "What if he had come into *my* room!"

Footprints in the garden indicated that the intruder had entered and left by the burglar-proof front gate. The ease with which he had accomplished this did not seem to bode well for the company's future, nor did the stream of bill collectors at its door. We were not surprised, therefore, when we got up one morning to find that the personnel of the burglar-alarm factory had quietly stolen away in the night, leaving behind only an old workbench and some scraps of copper wire.

Shortly after, Miss Winton and Miss Hopper's lease having expired, Mrs. Uchida decided they should pay more rent and half a year of it in advance. The English ladies, outraged, moved out in a huff. They were soon followed by the Halls, who were going to Tokyo, and from there to America, Mrs. Hall setting off in a pink sack-dress that stunned the local housewives into silence. In addition, the piano teacher announced she was giving up the ballroom, as Yoshiko's interest had shifted from ballet to hula hoops and she herself did all her teaching these days away from home.

Two elderly Japanese couples moved into the second- and third-floor rooms, respectively. The wives, who informed me they had heard shocking tales from the neighbors about what went on in the house, immediately set about creating an air of respectability by locking the front gate at nine in the evening. I was able to come and go as I pleased through the back gate, but the new policy inflicted great hardship on the mahjong-playing student, who was apprehended by the police one night as he was trying to climb over the wall to his own lodging.

I began to sense that an era was drawing to a close and that it was time to leave the mansion on the hill. The wife on the second floor attempted to interest me in a Noh-style singing group her husband belonged to, and sometimes brought me homemade pickled burdock root and little fishes boiled in soy sauce, but they were somehow not the same as Miss Winton's apricot pies. The piano was silent in the ballroom, "The White Peacock" no longer echoed in the night, and Stephan was not around to appreciate the wealth of insects that gathered on the front steps in the thin autumn sunlight to die.

Moreover, the tea-ceremony rooms, though picturesque and inexpensive, had begun to seem increasingly cramped, particularly as my collection of books expanded, and my roommate and I accordingly started making inquiries about lodgings elsewhere.

Meanwhile, a young Japanese medical student and his pregnant wife moved into our old rooms on the first floor. They did not look as though they could afford the rent, but Mrs. Uchida, who always spoke glowingly of new tenants and meanly of old ones, informed me that he was about to finish his internship and would then embark on a brilliant practice as an ear, nose, and throat specialist. Not long after, the wife went to a hospital to have her baby and an aunt arrived from the country to feed and take care of the husband during her absence. The aunt had had no experience of city living, and someone was always having to show her how to use the flush toilet or light the gas burner to heat up the bath. But she worked hard and, when her services were no longer needed, said goodbye to us all cheerily and returned to the country, confident no doubt that she had done her best for the young couple. It was some time before it became apparent what she had in fact done for them.

On returning to the house in the clear late autumn evenings, I had several times noticed an odor of gas that seemed to linger about the front gate, and other tenants had remarked on the same odor in parts of the garden. But for all our sniffing, we could never locate the source; the smell seemed to come down out of the sky, which was patently impossible. The mystery remained unsolved until the day when the gas man turned up with a monthly bill for the equivalent of over two hundred dollars.

All the living units in the house were on separate meters, and since none of the meters showed any abnormal increase except the one attached to the bath, we all assumed that it alone for some reason had suddenly gone haywire. An examination by the gas man revealed, however, that the meter was in perfect order and was merely recording in good faith the gas being used by the giant water heater next to the bath, which was also attached to it. As the gas man pointed out, the valve of the water heater was open all the way, and a copious stream of gas was pouring out of it and up the tall chimney that projected above the roof of the house.

Since my roommate and I had not been near the bath or the water heater for over half-a-year, we were completely out of the sordid squabble that followed. Mrs. Uchida made only the feeblest efforts to involve us in it, and then turned all her fury on the young medical student and his wife, whose country aunt in her bungling had apparently somehow opened the valve, unconscious of what she was doing. My roommate and I, having found other quarters in the meantime, moved out as unobtrusively as possible a few days after the discovery, amid sounds of weeping and mutual incriminations that issued from the downstairs rooms where Mrs. Uchida was parleying with her luckless tenants. For a moment the old mansion on the hill had regained its former distinction; once more, as in prewar days, it had one of the largest gas bills of any house in Kyoto. Who would eventually have to pay for this bizarre revival of past glory we did not stay around to find out.

1962

Translations

Poems by Jakushitsu Genkō

Jakushitsu Genkō (1290–1367) was one of the most distinguished poets of the *Gozan bungaku*, or "Literature of the Five Mountains," the body of prose and poetry written in Chinese by Japanese Zen monks of the Kamakura and Muromachi periods. Born in the Katsuyama region of Mimasaka in present-day Okayama Prefecture, he went to Kyoto at an early age and entered Zen training at Tōfuku-ji temple. Later he continued his studies in Kamakura and became a Dharma-heir of Yakuō Tokken (1245–1330), a disciple of the Chinese monk Lan-hsi Tao-lung.

In 1320 Jakushitsu went to China, then under Mongol rule, studying first at Mount T'ien-mu west of Hangchow and later at other Zen centers in southern China. After returning to Japan in 1326 he spent some thirty years in self-imposed obscurity, residing at a succession of country temples in the Okayama area, and later at various temples in the areas of modern Tottori, Shizuoka, and Shiga prefectures. In 1360 he was persuaded by Sasaki Ujiyori, constable of the province of Ōmi (present-day Shiga Prefecture), to settle down in a remote hilly site east of Lake Biwa. The following year a temple, Eigen-ji, was built for him there, where he lived until his death six years later. Students flocked to study under him, and the temple has remained an important center of Rinzai Zen study down to present times.

Jakushitsu clearly cherished the life of reclusion and refused all invitations that would oblige him to live in proximity to the centers of political power in Kyoto and Kamakura. Something of his attitude, and his distaste for

121

the great Zen establishments of the cities, can be seen in the following introduction to a poem that he wrote for a monk who shared his views:

In the first year of the Kōan era (1361) I came to live out my old age at the foot of Mount Hankō (Eigen-ji) in the province of Ōmi. At that time the attendant Sōrin Ka[1] came from the capital and, joining me in my drab and uneventful life, we passed the spring together and went on in that way till winter. I admired him for his unequaled innate qualities and the fact that he did not let his keen intelligence lead him astray. Instead he worked doggedly and determinedly at the search for enlightenment, pursuing his practice without wasting a single moment.

One night as we were seated around the fire leisurely chatting, he said to me, "When I was living in the temple with the other monks, I used to be so fond of reading old books that I would almost give up going to bed or forget to eat my meals. But then it suddenly occurred to me that trying to gain understanding through learning and the exercise of reason was in all probability merely prolonging my delusion, making my egoistical outlook worse than ever and laying foundations that would most likely lead me into a scramble for fame and profit. Was it not in fact the root cause that kept me bound to the realm of birth and death? How much better, I thought, if I put all study-desk matters out of my mind and contented myself with being a know-nothing, understand-nothing fellow, better if I left the temple, took a closer look at myself, and made enlightenment my only goal.

"It also occurred to me that the men of past times, even after they had come to understand the Great Truth, would

---

[1] *Sōrin Chūka, a monk of Tenryū-ji temple in Kyoto and Dharma-heir of Musō Soseki (1275–1350). By this time Musō Soseki was dead and Chūka had evidently become dissatisfied with the atmosphere at the temple. At this period many monks of the major Zen temples devoted more time to learning and literature than to religious training.*

still try to avoid becoming entangled in material things and everyday affairs. Some went off to the western mountains and never came back again. There were some whose whereabouts only became known because of the vegetable leaves that came drifting down the valley stream; some composed lines such as 'Vexing, vexing, worldly affairs, / better off in the mountains and hills! / Sleep under the vines and creepers, / let a heap of stones pillow your head.'[2] How different such men are from me and the likes of me, who do nothing but put our heads together, raise a rumpus, and let the seasons pass without accomplishing anything! So I vowed that from now on I would never return to the monastery, but would try to follow in the venerable footsteps of those wise recluses, spending the rest of my life on that alone."

I was more than ever impressed with the lofty character and wonderful vision of this man, not the kind that could ever be matched by our common run of mediocrities. So I wrote this poem to present to him.

Some three hundred and fifty poems in Chinese by Jakushitsu are preserved in a work compiled after his death, the *Eigen Jakushitsu Ōsho Goroku*. (I have used the annotated edition published in Kyoto in 1644.) Many of the poems are doctrinal in nature or otherwise rather specialized, but in the selection that follows, I have concentrated on works that reflect Jakushitsu's delight in his mountain retreats and his relations with friends and students.

---

[2] *The man who went off to the western mountains was the Chinese monk known as Abbot Liang, who originally lectured on Buddhist texts but later became a disciple of the Zen master Ma-tsu (709–788) and eventually disappeared into the mountains. The man whose hiding place was given away by vegetable leaves washing down the mountain stream was another disciple of Ma-tsu named Lung-shan. The author of the verses quoted was Lan-tsan, a monk who lived in a cave on Mount Heng and refused to leave his retreat even at the summons of the sovereign, Emperor Su-tsung (r. 756–762). The verses are from his long poem entitled "Song of Delighting in the Way."*

Though he shunned the cities, he was by no means averse to the company of others. On the contrary, like many recluses, he was acutely aware of the pleasures of companionship. His poetry is marked by warmth, lightness, and an engaging sense of humor, qualities that I hope will be apparent in the examples I have chosen. All the poems in my selection are in the four-line *chüeh-chü* or *zekku* form, the first two using a five-character line, the remainder, a seven-character line. The texts of the preface quoted above, and of all but one poem (No. 2), will be found in Harada Ryūmon's *Jakushitsu Genkō* (Tokyo: Shunjūsha, 1979), a work to which I am much indebted. For the text of No. 2, see Kitamura Sawakichi, *Gozan Bungaku Shikō* (Tokyo: Fuzambō, 1941), p. 296.

No. 1
Written on the Wall of a Mountain Retreat in
Shii Village

Water in the ravine flows down to the world of men,
clouds from the scarps pass on to other mountains.
Listen a while to the hidden birds chattering,
as though they're extolling the idleness of this
    countryside monk!

No. 2
Spending the Night at Kongō-ji
(There are several temples by the name Kongō-ji and it is
uncertain which is intended here.)

Often I come visiting this nearby temple.
We talk all night, never breaking off.
In this mountain village there are no signal drums.
When the window whitens, then we know it's
    dawn.

No. 3
Putting Up for the Night at Senkō-ji
(Senkō-ji was a temple in Onomichi on the Inland Sea.)

Ten years ago I visited my friend.
At sight of each other, we clasped hands, talked on
  like spring.
Who'd have thought tonight I'd sleep in his old
  room,
moonlight piercing the cold window, wind rocking
  the bamboo.

No. 4
Two Poems Written on the Wall at Mount Konzō
(At Konzōsan-ji temple in Tantō, Hyogo Prefecture;
second of two poems.)

Wind buffets the waterfall, sending me cold sounds.
From peaks in front, a moon rises, the bamboo
  window brightens.
Old now, I feel it more than ever—so good to be
  here in the mountains!
Die at the foot of the cliff and even your bones are
  clean.[3]

---

[3] *The last line is probably an allusion to the following poem by the
Chinese poet Wei Ying-wu (b. 736), who shared Jakushitsu's love of
the reclusive life:*

> *Visiting Someone on My Day Off but Not Finding Him Home*

> *(A variant version of the title makes it clear that the person
> visited was the poet-recluse Wang Chien.)*

> *Nine days racing around, one day free:*
> *I looked for you, didn't find you—now I go home empty-
>   handed.*
> *I've wondered why your poems seem to clean a man to his
>   bones:*
> *ah, your gate looks out on the cold brook, snow blankets
>   your hills.*

No. 5

My former attendant Zaiō came to visit me at my new place in Nobe (Shizuoka Prefecture). We sat around the fire pit all night talking of worthwhile matters. When he got ready to leave, I put together this little poem to express my gratitude.

I cut reeds for a new hut in a crook of the empty
   mountain.
You must have cared, coming so far to see me in my
   distant retreat.
We've burned up all the dry sticks, run out of words
   as well;
together we listen to the sound of icy rain pelting
   against the window.

No. 6
Spring Day, Mountain Walking

Head covered with wispy hair, twisted in silvery
   tufts:
can't tell if I'll be around to welcome spring next
   year.
Bamboo staff, straw sandals, lots of delights in
   the country;
looking at mountain cherries—how many trees
   does this make?

The poems quoted so far have reflected Jakushitsu's belief in the purifying nature of the mountain setting, its
power to "clean a man to his bones." Jakushitsu in fact
viewed the scenes of nature as the most eloquent guide to
enlightenment, as is seen in the two poems quoted next.
In these, he directs the student's attention to the elements
of the mountain landscape and calls upon him not only to

observe them, but to learn to identify with them, since they constitute a concrete embodiment of "this thing" that the student is seeking, the ultimate principle of Buddhism. As Jakushitsu puts it elsewhere in a short prose piece addressed to a student, "You are the green mountain, the green mountain is you!"[4]

No. 7
Two Poems to Show a Monk
(First of two poems)

This thing—I show it to you clear as can be!
No need to plot any special feats or exploits.
Breezes mild, sun warm, yellow warblers caroling;
spring at its height already there in the blossoming
   treetops.

No. 8
To Show to the Priest Named Son

A man of the Way comes rapping at my brushwood
   gate,
wants to discuss the essentials of Zen experience.
Don't take it wrong if this mountain monk's too
   lazy to open his mouth:
late spring warblers singing their heart out, a village
   of drifting petals.

The following poem is one of a series describing various Buddhas and bodhisattvas. This one is about the bodhisattva Manjushri or Monju, a fictional being who represents Supreme Wisdom. His statue is a regular fixture in

[4] *Kageki Hideo,* Gozan Shishi no Kenkyū *(Tokyo: Kasama Shoin, 1977), p. 136.*

Zen meditation halls, since it is his understanding that meditators are seeking to acquire. He is customarily portrayed riding on a lion and holding a "wordless sutra" and a sword, the latter used to cut off delusions. It was by awaking to his wisdom that the seven Buddhas of the past, the last being Shakyamuni, were able to attain enlightenment.

No. 9

> Haven't finished reading the last of your wordless
>   sutra,
> old sword, its blade dulled, uselessly held in your
>   hand,
> so many years stupidly seated on the back of the
>   golden-maned lion—
> who'd believe you were once teacher to the seven
>   Buddhas?

The last poem to be quoted was written to accompany a painting, a *chinsō*, or formal portrait, of Jakushitsu himself. The portrait, which no doubt showed Jakushitsu wearing full priestly robes and looking very solemn, was painted at the request of a woman lay-believer.

No. 10
At the Request of the Woman Lay-Believer Jigen

Who took these splendid robes of purple and gold,
wrapped them around the old fool's lump of red
    flesh?
When bystanders see him, I'm afraid they'll laugh—
better send him back to stay in his old green
    mountain!

Translated 1987

The Poem as Souvenir

Several years ago, when I was living in Wakayama, Japan, on the coast south of Osaka, I made a small collection of poems from the *Man'yōshū* dealing with Wakayama Prefecture, or the land of Ki, as it was called in ancient times. In the course of translating the poems, I became aware of the various things that a visit to Ki had meant to the *Man'yōshū* poets, most of them natives of the Nara area in Yamato: a journey over mountains; an opportunity to view famous spots such as Boy Mountain and Girl Mountain, two peaks on opposite sides of the Ki River that inspired numerous jeux d'esprit; to gaze in awe at the ocean and its offshore islands; perhaps to feel a twinge of homesickness; and to describe all these things in poems to show the people back in Nara. The poem, in other words, constituted a kind of souvenir brought home from the journey.

The *Man'yōshū*, or *Collection of Ten Thousand Leaves*, compiled around A.D. 759, is the earliest extant anthology of Japanese poetry. Its poets, though observing certain conventions, on the whole depicted the scenes of their journey with directness and simplicity, their works unmarred by the stereotyped responses and studied conceits of later poetry on the topic of travel and the natural landscape. Following is a selection of poems in *chōka* and *tanka* form, some by known writers, others anonymous, dealing with sights in various parts of Ki.

The Sea

No. 12

You have shown me Nojima,
the island I longed to see,
but you gather me no gems
from the deep-floored bay
of Agoné!

Waga horishi
Nojima wa misetsu
soko fukaki
Agone no ura no
tama so hiriwanu

Princess Nakatsusumera (d. 665)

No. 917

First year of Jinki (724), winter, tenth month, fifth day, written by Yamabe no Akahito when the Sovereign (Emperor Shōmu) visited the land of Ki.

From the fields of Saika	Yasumishishi
where we serve	waga ōkimi no
in the abiding place	tokomiya to
of our great lord	tsukaematsureru
who reigns serenely	Saikano yu
we turn to look out	sogai ni miyuru
at that island in the offing:	okitsushima
on its clean beaches	kiyoki nagisa ni
when the wind blows	kaze fukeba
the white waves thunder,	shiranami sawagi
and when tides go out	shio fureba
we gather seaweed there—	tamamo karitsutsu
from the age of the gods	kamiyo yori
honored thus,	shika zo tōtoki
island peak, Tamatsushima![1]	Tamatsushimayama

Yamabe no Akahito

---

[1] *Saika is at the bay of Wakanoura in present-day Wakayama City. Tamatsushima, or Jewel Island, is a small, rocky peak, now a part of the land but at this time an offshore island.*

No. 918   Envoy

Island in the offing—	Okitsushima
when the seaweed	ariso no tamamo
on its rocky shores	shiohi michite
is lost under tides returning,	kakuroi yukaba
we'll long for it then, I know!	omohoen kamo

No. 919   Envoy

In Wakanoura bay	Waka no ura ni
when the tide comes in,	shio michi kureba
sand spits sink from sight,	kata o nami
and the cranes, bound for	ashibe o sashite
reed banks,	
fly crying across the water	tazu naki wataru

No. 1215

Tamatsushima—	Tamatsushima
take a good look!	yoku mite imase
If the people at home in Nara	aoni yoshi
of the good gray soil	Nara naru hito no
should ask about it, what will you say?	machi towaba ika ni

Anonymous

No. 1217

I saw Tamatsushima	Tamatsushima
but it did no good—	mite shi yokeku mo
Once back in the capital	ware wa nashi
I'm sure	miyako ni yukite
I'll only want to see it again	koi maku omoeba

Anonymous

No. 1222

Tamatsushima—	Tamatsushima
I look at it, never tiring,	miredomo akazu
thinking how I might	ika ni shite
wrap it up,	
take it home	tsutsumi mochi yukamu
to show to someone	minu hito no tame
who's never seen it	

Fujiwara no Maetsukimi (dates uncertain)

No. 1221

Don't turn the rudder	Waga fune no
of my boat so soon—	kaji wa na hiki so
I've come from Yamato,	Yamato yori
avid for these sights	koi koshi kokoro
and I haven't seen enough of	imada akanaku ni
them yet!	

Fujiwara no Maetsukimi

No. 1219

In Wakanoura bay	Waka no ura ni
white waves leap up,	shiranami tachite
and in the evening	okitsukaze
cold with offshore winds	samuki yūbe wa
I think of Yamato	Yamato shi omoyu

Fujiwara no Maetsukimi

No. 1665

I am gathering rare stones	Imo ga tame
for my darling.	ware tama hiriu
You white waves in the offing,	oki he naru
bring me rare stones	tama yose mochi ko
from out there where you are!	okitsu shiranami

Anonymous

Mountains

No. 35

So this is it!	Kore ya kono
The much-named Boy Mountain	Yamato ni shite wa
on the road through Ki,	waga kouru
like the boy I long for	Kiji ni ari tou
back in Yamato—	na ni ou Se no yama

Princess Ahe (Empress Gemmei, r. 708–714)

No. 1193

Girl Mountain,	Se no yama ni
with Boy Mountain	tada ni mukaeru
right across the river—	Imo no yama
has she said he can come	koto yuruse ya mo
visit her?	
There's a plank bridge	uchihashi watasu
spanning the flow!	

Anonymous

No. 1208

Longing for that girl	Imo ni koi
I cross over Boy Mountain	waga koe yukeba
envying him—	Se no yama no
he needn't long,	Imo ni koizute
his Girl Mountain right in front of him!	aru ga tomoshisa

Anonymous

No. 1212

Past Até	Ate sugite
to Mount Itoka,	Itoka no yama no
and may its cherries	sakurabana
not shed their blossoms	chirazu aranamu
till I come again on my way back home!	kaeri kuru made

Anonymous

No. 1213

Nagusayama
is nothing but a name!
It will not comfort
one part in a thousand
of these pains of love I feel![2]

Nagusayama
koto ni shi ari keri
waga koi no
chie no hitoe mo
nagusamenaku ni

Anonymous

---

[2] *The poem plays on the name of the mountain on the coast just south of Wakayama, Mount Nagusa, and the verb* nagusamu, *to comfort or soothe.*

Another View of the Journey

No. 543

Written at the request of a woman so she could give it to one of the men accompanying the emperor on his journey to the land of Ki in winter, the tenth month of the first year of Jinki (724).

Husband I love,	Ōkimi no
numbered among the guardians,	miyuki no ma ni ma
men of eighty clans,	mononofu no
who've set out	yasotomo no o to
with our great lord	ide yukishi
on his royal journey,	utsukushi tsuma wa
going by way of Karu road,	ama tobu ya
wild geese in the sky,	Karu no michi yori
gazing on jewel-chorded	tamatasuki
Mount Unebi,	Unebi o mitsutsu
from there entering the road	asamo yoshi
to Ki,	
Ki of the good hemp skirts—	Kiji ni iritachi
now you must be crossing over	Matsuchiyama
Mount Matsuchi.	koyuramu kimi wa
And as you watch the yellow	momijiba no
leaves	
fluttering and scattering,	chiritobu mitsutsu
you think no more of me,	mutsumashimi
much as I loved you.	ware wa omowazu
Instead you're thinking,	kusamakura
grass for a pillow,	tabi o yoroshi to
how fine the journey is.	omoitsutsu
That's what you're doing—	kimi wa aramu to
I've an inkling	asoso ni wa
of how things go,	katsu wa shiredomo

and yet I can't simply stand by
in silence.
I wish I could follow
in the footsteps
of your journey—
a thousand times
I think of it—
but weak woman that I am,
if the sentries along the road
should question me,
how would I answer?
I stand here perplexed,
not knowing what to do.

Kasa no Kanamura

shikasu ga ni
modae araneba
waga seko ga
yuki no ma ni ma ni
owamu to wa
chie ni omoedo
tamayame no
waga mi ni shi areba
michimori no
towamu kotae o
iiyaramu
sube o shira ni to
tachite tsumazuku

No. 544   Envoy

Rather than be left behind,   Okure ite
to stay here longing,   koitsutsu arazu wa
I wish we could be   Ki no kuni no
the Boy and Girl mountains   Imo Se no yama ni
in the land of Ki!   aramashi mono o

No. 545   Envoy

If I should go after you,   Waga seko ga
following your traces,   ato fumi motome
pushing my way along,   oi yukaba
the guards at the pass to Ki   Ki no sekimori i
might stop me for all I know!   todometemu ka mo

Four Poems from the Land of Ki

From the *Kakinomoto no Hitomaro Collection*, a collection of poems written by, or perhaps merely collected and reworked by, Kakinomoto no Hitomaro (active c. 700).

No. 1796

The beach where	Momijiba no
I romped with the children	suginishi kora to
hand in hand—	tazusawari
children who scattered like	asobishi iso o
autumn leaves—	
Seeing it makes me sad!	mireba kanashi mo

No. 1797

A rough shore	Shioke tatsu
where the sea spray rises,	ariso ni wa aredo
but I've come because	yuku mizu no
it's all I have left of my loved	suginishi imo ga
one,	
gone like the flowing water	katami to so koshi

No. 1798

Kuroushi bay,	Inishie ni
black as leopard flower seeds,	imo to waga mishi
that long ago my love and I	nubatama no
looked on together—	Kuroushigata o
seeing it now, I'm lonely	mireba sabushi mo

No. 1799

I'll dye my robe	Tamatsushima
with the fine sands	iso no ura mi no
from the bay-rounding beach	manago ni mo
of Tamatsushima,	nioite yukana
knowing my love has walked	imo ga furekemu
on them	

Translated 1988

About the Author

Burton Watson was born in New Rochelle, New York, in 1925. He graduated from Columbia College in 1949, after majoring in Chinese; in 1956, he received a doctorate in Chinese from Columbia University. From 1951 to 1955 he was a graduate student in Chinese studies at Kyoto University in Japan and has subsequently spent much of his time in Japan. He has taught at Columbia, Stanford, and Kyoto universities and was formerly professor of Chinese at Columbia University. Since 1973 he has lived in Japan and devoted his time to translation work. He has published over thirty books on, or translations from, Chinese and Japanese literature. In 1979 he received the Gold Medal Award from the Translation Center at Columbia University. The anthology of ancient and modern Japanese poetry, *From the Country of Eight Islands* (Doubleday & Co., 1981; Columbia University Press, 1986), which he edited and translated with Hiroaki Sato, won the 1982 PEN translation prize.

Book design by Nick Gregoric.

Text set in Trump Mediaeval and Optima on a
Linotron 202 by Wilsted & Taylor, Oakland, California.

Printed on acid-free paper and Smyth sewn by
Malloy Lithographing, Inc., Ann Arbor, Michigan.